QUICK
······ POETRY ······
ACTIVITIES

By Jacqueline Sweeney

SCHOLASTIC
PROFESSIONAL BOOKS

NEW YORK ■ TORONTO ■ LONDON ■ AUCKLAND ■ SYDNEY

For Russ Aldrich–

Whose music speaks a poem.

Extensive research failed to locate the author of "Look Closely," Morton Marcus.

"A Tale for Dien Tamaela" from *The Voice in the Night: Complete Poetry and Prose of Chairil Anwar*, translated by Burton Raffel, Revised Edition. Copyright © 1993 by the Center for International Studies Ohio University. Reprinted by permission of Burton Raffel.

"Edible", "If My Face Were Outer Space", "Family Trees" and "Food Music" by Jacqueline Sweeney. Copyright © 1994 by Jacqueline Sweeney. Reprinted by permission of Marian Reiner.

"Being a Kite" and "Choose a Color" by Jacqueline Sweeney. Copyright © 1993 by Jacqueline Sweeney. Reprinted by permission of Marian Reiner.

"I'm So Mad I Could Scream" by William Cole. Reprinted by permission of the author.

"How to Eat a Poem" and "Landscape" from *A Sky Full of Poems* by Eve Merriam. Copyright © 1964, 1970, 1973, 1986 by Eve Merriam. Reprinted by permission of Marian Reiner for the author.

"December 21" Reprinted by permission of Atheneum Books for Young Readers, an imprint of Simon & Schuster's Children's Publishing Division, from *Something New Begins* by Lilian Moore.

Designed by Joan Gazdik Gillner/Judith Harlan, Editorial Services and Publication Management

Cover design and illustration by Vincent Ceci and Frank Maiocco

Interior illustration by Rowan Barnes-Murphy

ISBN: 0–590–49767–7

Table of Contents

ACKNOWLEDGMENTS

I'd like to thank the administration, students and staff of the following New York Schools: Pawling Elementary, Cairo Elementary, Gardnertown Fundamental Magnety School of Newburgh, Traver Road Elementary of Pleasant Valley, La Grange Elementary, Kent Primary of Carmel, Donald P. Sutherland, Green Meadow, Red Mill and Belltop of East Greenbush, Central Valley Elementary, Upper Nyack Elementary, and Rondout Valley Intermediate School.

A special thanks goes to Rita Sturgis, Linda Valenchis, Bettie McMasters, Joyce Curtis, and Pat Williams for extra assistance with permissions, and to Dr. Kathryn May for her insightful suggestions concerning rewrites.

An overdue thank-you goes to Kay Stamer of Green County Council on the Arts for her yearly support of my workshops in Greene County Schools, and my constant gratitude to Marian Reiner for her support and good advice. I'm also grateful to my children, Matt and Gabby Piperno, for their unfailing honesty in response to my work and questions, as well as to all the children who had the personal courage to write the many moving poems contained here.

Thanks to the following students who have given permission to reprint their poems:

Michael Telesca, Anna Ditton, Kate Slotwinski, Jun Sun, Thomas McCaffery, Josh Berkowits, Elisa Brotherhood, Alex Gomez, Alesia Borgen, Corrie Pickston, Dermot Donnelly, Michael Viglante, Warren Agostinoni, Lija Kurens, Marissa Betro, Sean Donovan, John Fitzsimmons, Derek Kruiger, Meghan Miller, Billie Davies, Chris Hart, Ashly Herman, Katie Biamonte, Katie Schmand, Colleen Kutner, David Suitto, Jen Buckworth, Sarah Winne, Jennifer Gibson, Andrea Tonkin, Nicole Phelps, Amy Beyor, Alexis Domenicucci, John Sorriento, Stefanie Perl, Danielle Pitts, Abby Mennerich, Melissa Shields, Iyamide House, Justin Saglibene, Erica Finizio, Luciano Valdivia, David Riley, Diana D'Muro, Kelly McBride, Brandon Alvarez, Paul Plekon, Kyra Johnston, Billy Parke, Sara Sairitupa, Tommy Miller, Kris McGowan, Sarah Delena, Robert Erhardt, Jaime DelGrosso, Jillian Utter, Jessica Gallo, Brandon Nikola, Jason Chipkin, Steven Strong, James Kimma, Alissa Stoever, Christelle Munnelly, Rebecca Commerford, Andrew Murphy, Michelle Leo, Vincent Galvin, Brinton Moore, Randi Licari, Halsey McGowan, Kathy Lee, Laura Lynn, Maria Schmitt, Anja Brand, Melissa Suter, Chrissy McCormack, Jeff Renwich, Jaclyn Gomez, Amy Forzano, Nicole DePompeis, A.J. Koola, Amanda da Silva, Laura De Fabbia, Allison Wooden, Tyler Johnson, Lauren Palladina, Kyle Lyon, Jonathan Place

Extensive research failed to locate the following student authors:

Jarred Kodran, Michael Gennett, Mulubirhan Kassahun, Aimee James, Michael Sherrill, Renee Byrd, Wendi Tomaszek, Tranise Brown, Sharon Smolen, Richard DiStefano, Benjamin Jenkins, Terrence Brooks, Chris Wilson, Rinah Davis, Frank Richardson, Asheda Walker, Helen Nonge, Paul Deeny, Matthew Kline, Kim Kelly, Patricia Nagy, Edward Bowling, Jennifer Banach, John Damian, Rachael Malach, Marcus Banks, Alana Descera, Erika Newson, Sarah Winner, Fames Ridgway, Hollw Weidenbacker, Suzanne Potts, Jessica Horvath, Laurie Ford, Christopher Latka, John Greet, Naomi Lager, Jessica Nolfo, Nicole Satterwhite, Chrissy George, Adam Wightman, Nicole Orio, Wendy Morales, Sheri Olin, Adam Bloom, Lou Ernst, Amy Quesnel, Travis Gale, Jennifer Cichocki, Myra Sanchez, Matthew Sataloff, Ken Stanhope, Chris Damiana, Michelle Raulf, Timothy McCormick, Ivan Silva, Michael O'Donnell, Elizabeth Morris, Nick Bigelow, Trissa Therien, Victoria Vanzo

Introduction

I've discovered over the years that many teachers are hesitant to spend even a few days teaching poetry in their classrooms either because they have had so little association with it in their own experiences as students, or the experiences they did have were negative. More often than not, the teachers who do get an opportunity to teach poetry are bound by the confining time frame of tight curriculums. A time problem for some, poetry's terrain poses still another problem for others. "I don't know where to begin," many teachers confide. "I don't know where to look for good children's poetry—or what poems to choose!"

My initial response to questions like these was a Scholastic Professional Book, *Teaching Poetry, Yes You Can*, which contains many poems by both established poets and children, and offers step-by-step advice about how to introduce poetry to any classroom through structured lessons in simile, imagery, strong verbs, nouns, adjectives, onomatopoeia, alliteration, refrain, and more.

But what about those in-between times when a teacher and class have only a few free moments before lunch or at the end of the day? What fills those dreadful lulls on field trips, or when the bus is late, or when there's a twenty minute wait in some museum line? Every teacher has a horror story about being stranded with twenty-five hungry youngsters on a stalled bus, or, God forbid, an elevator! And what about those moments when no materials are available: no pencils, paper, or books. No snacks!?

My response to these questions is this book: *Quick Poetry Activities (You Can Really Do!)*, designed not only to fill those expected and unexpected moments that comprise a classroom teacher's daily regimen, but to help turn these moments into enjoyable, creative experiences for *both* the children and their teacher.

Since I spend so much time each year in elementary school classrooms, I'm aware of how a teacher's schedule can change at a moment's notice from day to day, and how flexible he or she must remain in order to cope with the demands of state mandated agendas versus allotted classroom hours.

With this in mind, I've organized the poetry exercises in this book for teachers to use in numerous ways: as time fillers with solid language arts benefits, as supplements to a whole-language curriculum, or simply to stimulate new ideas and ways of thinking in a fun and interesting manner.

But what about the teacher who wants poetry lessons she can actively use as part of her curriculum; lessons she can expand upon to reinforce specific skills and themes? This book can surely be used in this capacity, and the strategies contained herein have been designed to meet both long-term and short-term curriculum goals. A teacher might wish to take the chapter on Self-Portraits, for example, and use it as a one-time, quick poem activity where a child's face (or arms, legs, hands, feet, etc.) is described using funny and imaginative language. He or she might also employ "Portraits" as a device for children to learn and use the vocabulary of the skeletal system, or circulatory system, etc. I've often introduced this chapter with a short discussion of the history of portrait painting—how we'd never know what George Washington looked like if it weren't for portrait painters

because cameras hadn't been invented when George was alive.

Once the simple method of each poem activity is understood, it can be used over and over again to inspire children to write about many related themes. Over the years I've come to greatly respect the abilities of teachers to take what works for *them* from my curriculum offerings and add insightful ideas and concepts of their own—expanding the content range of a lesson, and thereby adapting my ideas to better suit the particular needs of each class.

When I visit a school as writer-in-residence for a week, I'm often asked to work with four classes of the same grade level. As I discover each class's collective attention span and level of comprehension, it rarely fails that I must offer the same lesson four different ways. For example, I might pace the material much faster for one class by dropping some of my introductory remarks and immediately reading one of the poems, or I might slowly introduce a lesson and offer more of its poem samples to a class that's capable of more sustained listening. Since I offer many different poems for each activity (some by adults, some by children), I rarely use them all, but rather choose one or two poems that I feel will work best with the interests, age, and emotional  level of each class. And as every teacher knows, each class, though comprised of the same aged children, is different.

Every class assumes its own mood, tone, and energy level, and though a teacher's pacing must be altered throughout any given day to accommodate—morning, before lunch, after lunch, and after 'specials'—energy and attention capacities, there's always that undefined element that gives every class its own stamp. And this is what I've designed *Quick Poetry Activities (You Can Really Do!),* to address. I've tried to offer a variety of activities and sample poems so that teachers might comfortably choose what works for them—to drop parts of some activities and supplement oth-

ers—to best suit the needs of the ever-increasing classroom varieties second through fifth graders provide. I've also tried to design a book that can be used often in a variety of subject areas throughout the year.

Linda Golden, a fourth grade teacher from Rosendale Elementary School in upstate New York, told me she began to recognize the versatility as well as whole language possibilities for poetry in her classroom a few years ago, and now uses poetry—not just once a year—but at appropriate moments all through the year. She expressed keen interest in a book filled with poem activities that can be done with her class on the spot, either verbally or in written format; anytime a convenient moment allows.

I believe poetry is a thoughtful way for children to explore everyday environments through the use of their senses and feelings. It provides a vehicle that is so versatile; it can offer insight into those odd, funny moments we encounter every day. Poetry assists children to make eloquent, daily commentaries about the joys and sorrows happening in their lives, but it doesn't stop there. It can also suggest worlds of subjects for children to explore, such as the life cycles of plants, animal habitats, newspaper headlines, imaginative kingdoms, biography and autobiography, or the personification of kites, toasters, dwellings, blades of grass, sunsets, snow, etc. etc. The list of possible subjects for poetry goes on and on. I hope this book will help teachers feel more comfortable using poetry in their classrooms and begin to view poetry as a teaching companion—a delightful means to a solid educational end.

And one thing more: I hope the explorations in this book allow teachers to discover, as I have, that poetry, ultimately, is a language of the heart and—whatever its subject— encourages children to affirm their existence in their own terms, not only to themselves, but to their families, teachers, other students—the world! Poetry is a way to say: "I'm here. Listen to what I have to tell you." Notice the humble assertion of eight-year-old Alesia:

> ### THE SILLY CAT
> I am a cat that is very quiet.
> It seems like I am not in the house.
> I don't make a bump,
> I don't make a thump.
> They forgot about me.
> I am as quiet as a plant out in the fields.
> No one knows I am there.
> I am yellow like wheat.
> It seems like I am not there.
> I AM.
> I'm there.
> — Alesia Borgen, Grade 2

When I sometimes feel discouraged in my work as a writer and teacher, children like Alesia remind me, with clear, poignant eloquence why I'm still here, teaching poetry, after all these years.

Some Initial Concepts

THE 'LIKE WHAT' LIST:

The building blocks for all my poetry programs are similes and metaphors. I introduce these concepts during my first encounters with every class (grades one–twelve) along with the power of colors and sense mixing (synaesthesia). I describe a typical first encounter with a class in detail in *Teaching Poetry, Yes You Can,* but I think it's important to briefly introduce these concepts to you because I will be referring to them through-

out this book as devices to both facilitate your students' use of the poetry strategies contained here as well as deepen their overall writing experience.

I initially present the technique of simile in the form of what I call the 'Like What' List.

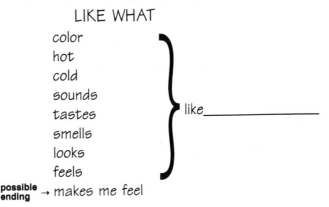

LIKE WHAT

color
hot
cold
sounds
tastes
smells
looks
feels

possible ending → makes me feel

} like_____

I teach students this list very quickly by posting it somewhere in the classroom and suggesting a mnemonic device for them to use to recall it when the list is not around:

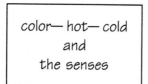

color— hot— cold
and
the senses

I also tell them to count each sense on their fingers as they reconstruct it for themselves either on paper or in their minds.

I suggest "makes me feel" as a possible ending for poems when an ending is not readily forthcoming, but I also stress that "makes me feel" can be used anywhere in a poem. It needn't be a standard ending. Wherever it is used, I find its addition to student thinking often deepens the level of any poetry experience for them.

HOW THE 'LIKE WHAT' LIST WORKS:

Anything can be taken through the 'Like What' list whether it's something concrete (a thing) or something abstract (a thought or feeling). For example, the floor may be as tan as a whale's tongue, or rough like a bumpy road. Peace might be blue as a glacier in Alaska or taste like hot chocolate after a hard day at school.

(Notice my substitution of "as" for "like" at times.)

The point of the 'Like What' or 'Simile' list is to offer children a reference source that constantly encourages imagery and careful word choice as realistic devices for transforming any aspect of experience into poetry. It's important to stress that your children have choices to make and should use only the parts of the list that work for each poem (and individual!).

POEM MODELS:

With each writing activity I'll frequently include a poem model designed for easy adaptation to the variations in individual lesson plans. Remember: **No poem model is written in stone.** As I encourage you to change words or phrases in the model according to your ideas for format, encourage your students to cross out words in a model that don't suit their meanings and to substitute words of their own wherever necessary. The purpose of a poem model is to teach children about *possibility* in structure and content, and ultimately to free them to create new structures and meanings of their own. For example, no poem model could possibly inspire the mood and feeling of the following poem by eight-year-old Lija:

> A WILD CAT
>
> At home I am like a wild
> cat. And when the floor is
> slippery I run like a jaguar
> and I stop like a sentence.
> — Lija Kurens, Grade 2

Poem models can be typed or written out and photocopied as lessons either instead of or in conjunction with being put on the blackboard or overhead projector. When time permits, a poem idea can be explored together as a class collaboration. The collaborative poem then becomes an experienced model for students to refer to when writing their own poems. I suggest you create a separate folder of *Poem Models* for student reference throughout the year—whenever free time is available. And always encourage your children to change your model whenever necessary to make their poems sing out with their own voices and styles. Praise their attempts to be new and different. After brainstorming a long list of 'objects' and verbs and adjectives for a poem activity with a fifth grade recently, I told them, "Here are some words you might choose from, and here is a model to help you start or give you ideas. But it's your job to put in the magic and make it a poem. Only you can do that." And they did.

BASIC PROCEDURE:

I recommend the following basic procedure when using *Quick Poetry Activities (You Can Really Do!)* (obviously steps may be cut as circumstances and time dictate, just as any poetry activity may be savored slowly and expanded into an entire poetry lesson within your curriculum):

1. Present topic

2. Brainstorm related ideas

3. Offer a model (verbal, a handout, on the board)

4. Share your students' poems

Remember that with every poem activity you do with your class, you are generating models of your own to offer as samples to subsequent groups.

POEMS AS STORIES:

As you begin to explore *Poetry Activities*, you'll begin to notice that some activities lend themselves more easily to a story format, for example, "If I Were from Outer Space," "Music Poems" and "Kingdoms." Writing a poem as a 'story' does not compromise the nature of a poem, nor sabotage the purpose of this book. Words sometimes need to spill out as stories before they can be constructed into poems. But poems often tell stories in their own right. It's the careful choice of words and use of language (similes, metaphors) that sets a poem apart from prose. In fact, many small stories are often structured to look like poems (I tell young children to make their words look "skinny" on the page); so the reverse—a poem that looks like a story—is more than acceptable to satisfy the purpose of this book.

The most important thing is that children are not only writing, but learning to think of poetry as a process that includes their choosing a subject, brainstorming its components, and combining their senses and objective vision to create imagery. Some of the best stories published today either contain poetic elements or started out as poems. So unless you have specific poetry curriculum goals in mind, allow your students a generous interchange between story and poem.

CHILDREN'S SAMPLE POEMS:

No matter how well presented a poetry lesson is, nothing inspires children more than hearing the poems of other children. Because a sample poem written in the style of the lesson just presented is the best inspiration, I've tried to include a variety of children's sample poems whenever possible.

With some poem activities I've included a large number of children's sample poems because the ideas might inspire a wider focus or invite more variations in poetic style; and I believe the more ideas presented through the work of others, the better the response from the class at hand. With some lessons I've deliberately included more poems than you might wish to use in a single presentation, but I feel it's important to offer options for you to choose from. One poem may contain a theme or idea that's perfect for the current interests or imagination of one class, but not for another; so choose from the samples presented according to your personal classroom needs.

A NOTE ABOUT WHOLE LANGUAGE AND INTEGRATED CURRICULA:

I believe *Poetry Activities* work well in any whole-language curriculum because they are so versatile. The "If I Were . . ." format, for example, can be used in a variety of subject areas ranging from the study of art to outer space. And the same activity can project a serious tone or a humorous one, depending on a teacher's presentation. Whatever the approach, new information is being unearthed—as in the brainstorming process—and subject areas broken down and explored—as in the poem writing process. Whether it be the expansion of dictionary skills, explorations of character through art, vision through music, vocabularies for outer space, famous names in history, or food, these poem strategies will successfully enrich *any* curriculum. In fact, I'm hoping teachers will find this book varied enough to contain something for everyone.

Easy Beginnings

LOOKING ATS:

"Looking Ats" is an excellent way for children to begin their poetry explorations because it is grounded in the familiar world of concrete, everyday objects and easily introduces them to the concept of simile.

1. Ask each child to choose an object—any object—animate or inanimate—inside the classroom or outside—something big as the moon or tiny as dust-balls under the bed.

2. Next ask them to close their eyes and look at the object in their minds.

3. When they've visualized the object to their satisfaction, ask your children to write their object's name on top of a piece of paper (lined or unlined). This is the title of the poem.

4. I suggest you post the 'Like What' List (see "Some Initial Concepts") somewhere in your classroom or put it on the board for easy reference, and then ask your students to write about their objects choosing at least two 'Like Whats' (similes) that they feel work best to describe them.

5. Remind your children to use their imaginations; if an object is 'green like grass,' ask them to think of some other 'green' that is surprising and interesting, or to give details to make their grass special, such as "green as young grass bent low by a spring breeze."

6. Next you might wish to read some children's sample "Looking At" poems to inspire reticent writers.

7. As they write, encourage your children to offer more details. For example, if one child writes that something is yellow as a flower, you might ask, "What kind of flower? Where is it—in a vase on a table—in someone's back yard?" After these questions you might see a yellow flower become a buttercup in a jelly jar or a bunch of dandelions dotting a summer hillside.

8. Finally, allow students to hear each others' poems. I prefer to have children read their own poems, but time may not permit—so you read them. Even if you share a few poems at a time over a period of several days, it will be worth it.

BIRDS

I like
birds
their wings
are colorful
and their beaks
are
like long orange stickers
their eyes
are
as tiny as snail's eyes
and
their
feet
are
small
they have long toenails
and some look funny.
What I like most is their
bulgy eyes.
— Jarred Kodran, Grade 3

A star travels all over the
world it lights up like the sun.
And if you are out for dinner
a star has 5 people in it. And
when it moves all over they meet
in the middle.
Then they are friends.
— Marissa Betro, Grade 2

FROG

The frog's feet are like sticky bubble
gum floating through the sky
and the frog's eyes look like eggs
burning on the stove and his stomach
is like a ball popping in the air.
— Ivan Silva, Grade 4

SCHOOL

School is not fun.
We do a ton of work.
It feels like an elephant sat on
Your head.
Some teachers are mean as a big
Grizzly bear.
You get as tired as a big old
Push broom.
It feels like I walked fifty miles
With tires on my feet.
— Michael Gennett, Grade 4

THE CLARINET

The clarinet is dark and mysterious like the unknown
rivers of Africa.
The clarinet is tall and proud like the graceful
towers of France.
The clarinet lifts and carries me, slow and swaying a gentle
wind, dancing,
through the delicate leaves of a weeping willow, crying for
its lost soul.
It takes me to many countries and lands like the frozen soil of
the Alaskan tundra.
All of these places are dark, mysterious, tall, proud, slow, swaying and gentle
LIKE ME.

— Mulubirhan Kassahun, Grade 5

THE BLIZZARD

Today we had a blizzard.
The snow was like white crayons all over.
I will go sledding.
I will have a lot of fun.
It will be like sledding on the clouds.
Then it will start snowing again.
My mother will call me in.
I will tell her I rode on the clouds.
I will tell her icicles are like swords
hanging from the sky.

— Aimee James, Grade 4

A BUTTERFLY DANCER

I see myself moving like a
Butterfly in so many ways. I
See myself as a little butterfly
In a bright blue sky. Then I
See a little girl dancing around.
I started dancing in the bright
Blue sky. People saw me glowing
With color pink, purple and
Green. I'm dancing to the singing
of birds putting their children
to sleep. I wish I was a dancer
so I could love a child who
Dances in the street.
      I love being a butterfly
            Dancer.

— Iyamide House, Grade 4

THE OLDEST THING IN THE WORLD

This is one of those activities where the children's sample poems provide the inspiration. It is a special favorite of teachers of younger children (grades two and three), who like to have the children 'sound out' each word from our word list as it is put on the board.

1. Put the following list of words on the board:

oldest	longest	tallest
smallest	flattest	softest
curliest	brightest	sharpest
darkest	scariest	furriest

2. Next choose one of the words and brainstorm ideas for it with the children; for example, the "smallest" thing in the world. I encourage many different responses as the class brainstorms together, and try to make the children feel as free as possible to express their own ideas verbally, so they will do the same thing when it's time to write. And if creative examples aren't forthcoming, I prompt the class with ideas of my own:

"The smallest thing in the world is _____

> an ant's eye
> a ladybug's spots
> a crumb
> a germ, etc.

3. It's frequently helpful to put a model on the board prior to reading the children's sample poems.

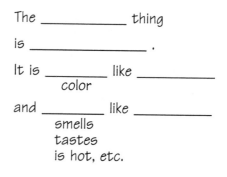

The _____ thing

is _____ .

It is _____ like _____
       color

and _____ like _____
    smells
    tastes
    is hot, etc.

Be sure to direct your class to the 'Like What' list!

4. Finally, read the children's sample poems.

CHILDREN'S SAMPLE POEMS:

The oldest thing is a fossil.
Fossils are white like paper.
They are as big as a school.
Some are thick like tree
trunks.
Some are thin like twigs.
When I think of fossils it's
like the world is a pebble.
— Michael Telesca, Grade 2

THE CURLIEST THING IN THE WORLD
The curliest thing is a snail shell.
And a perm like my grandmother's.
It feels like a rock going in circles.
— Michael Sherril, Grade i

THE BIGGEST THING
The sea is the biggest thing.
Fish live in the sea.
People fish with their fishing poles.
When snow drops in the water it melts.
Sometimes rainbows are on top of the water.
Renee does not like the sea monsters.
Turtles live in the sea.
— Renee Byrd, Grade 1

OLD PEOPLE
The oldest thing is God.
God is the oldest thing in the
city. He is older than Jesus.
My grandmother is old as my
grandpa. My dad is older
than me. My grandma has
a big crack in her foot
and it's skinny. This
is what happens
when you are old.
— David Suitto, Grade 2

THE SMALLEST THING
The smallest thing is salt.
It feels rough like the dirt on
the ground.
It sounds like the sea blowing.
It makes me feel good
like a cat.
— Wendi Tomaszek, Grade 1

THE LONGEST THING

The longest thing is the sky.
It's so long that it takes up the
whole world.
At night the stars fill up the
sky.
It looks like the stars are
floating in the sky.
— Elizabeth Morris, Grade 2

The Curliest thing in the world is curly hair.
It is very, very curly.
It is like Cinderella's sister's hair.
The curliest hair is pretty.
The curliest hair tap dances.
Curly hair is like spaghetti all curled up on a plate.
— Tranise Brown, Grade 1

The longest thing in the world is an air
craft carrier. It is grey like a great
white shark. It makes a growling sound
like an angry bear.   It
looks like a grown-up whale swimming
slowly through the sea. It is flat like
a new desk.   It makes me feel
angry like King Kong. It
makes me feel like I want to go on it.
    It makes me feel scared like a
rabbit that just saw a wolf.
— Michael O'Donnell, Grade 2

BEING A COLOR:

Before I begin this activity I ask the children to imagine that the color, bright orange, is filling up their bodies. Then I ask if it makes them feel hot or cold. Next we verbally share their responses as a class using the concept of the 'Like What' List to create interesting similes. I usually offer at least two examples, one from fantasy and one from everyday:

(fantasy) "Orange makes me feel hot like swimming in lava."

(everyday) "Orange makes me feel cold like picking up snow and feeling it drip into my sleeve."

It's a good idea to brainstorm in this manner with different colors until you feel the class is ready for the following model:

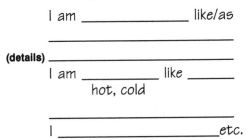

Before the children begin writing, it's a good idea to remind them again of the "green as grass" trap. Tell them to make a picture that's new and offer examples:

"Green as spring grass with one trickle of dew rolling down its pale stem."

or

"Green as the lining of my dad's best jacket or the emerald in the necklace of a queen."

CHILDREN'S SAMPLE POEMS:

COLORS

I'm red like fire.
I am yellow like the moon.
  When I'm mad I'm orange.
  And when I'm sad I'm blue.
  When somebody pulls my hair,
  I feel like a flower getting
      picked.
  When I'm hot I feel like
      the sun.
        — Sharon Smolen, Grade 3

BEAUTIFUL BLUE

I am blue
like a
River flooding
into a creek.
I feel like
a river being
sailed on.
I also feel
like Siamese
eyes looking
at somebody.
It makes
Me feel very
　　　Happy.
— John Fitzsimmons, Grade 2

SNAKE

I
am
black
as
night
it
is
spooky
out
I
can
hear
the
flowers
　　talking
I
can
hear
the
raccoons
I
　　am
　　scared
　　I
　　am
　　a
　　Snake
— Sean Donovan, Grade 2

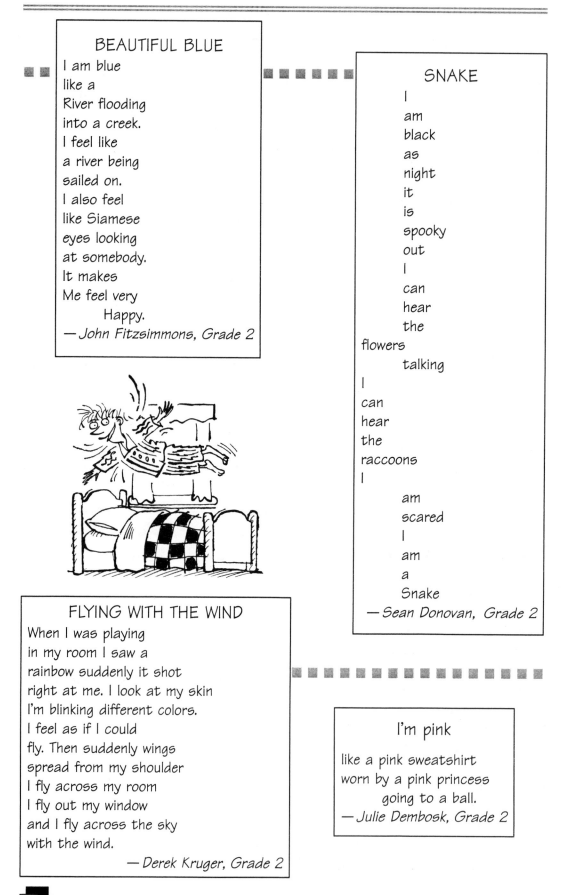

FLYING WITH THE WIND

When I was playing
in my room I saw a
rainbow suddenly it shot
right at me. I look at my skin
I'm blinking different colors.
I feel as if I could
fly. Then suddenly wings
spread from my shoulder
I fly across my room
I fly out my window
and I fly across the sky
with the wind.
　　　　— Derek Kruger, Grade 2

I'm pink

like a pink sweatshirt
worn by a pink princess
　　going to a ball.
— Julie Dembosk, Grade 2

BEAUTIFUL BLUE

I'm blue like a beautiful cloud racing across
the sky. I'm beautiful blue like blue
blossoms people are stepping on. I roar like
the most mean tiger in the world. I roar like
a heart that is breaking. I feel sad because
my cats died that I loved. I feel sad because
my family left without me.

— Corrie Pickston, Grade 2

RED

I'm red like a strawberry
Rolling down a hill.
I sound like a person
thumping down the stairs.
I feel so free
Growing under the golden sun,
Waving through the green grass—
Polka dots of the finest seeds.

— Anna Ditton, Grade 3

MY DAY

I am green blue like a tree with
a blue jay laying eggs. I feel
my friend's friendship between us.
I sound like a rat when I
rumple my paper. I look like a
pink gander and a swan swimming. Daylight makes me feel like
a great big pool in the middle of a
hot summer. Every day I swim in
deer tears made by a deer shot
in hunters ridge. When I see my
friend sick I feel like staying at
her house until she is better. I
feel like going to my friend's house
and staying for a whole year.

— Meghan Miller, Grade 2

CLAPPING COLORS:

This activity can provide an excellent break for the younger child who especially needs frequent shifts of both body and mind in order to remain focused.

1. Begin by clapping four steady beats:

(clap)	(clap)	(clap)	(clap)
(clap)	(clap)	(clap)	(clap)

2. As you continue clapping, speak in rhythm:

(teacher) "I'm thinking of a color   and it
      (clap)   (clap)   (clap)   (clap)

"   is green
      (clap)   (clap)   (clap)   (clap)

"   Like what?
      (clap)   (clap)   (clap)   (clap)

"   Like the big eyes of my cat"
      (clap) (clap) (clap) (clap)

3. Call out the name of a student (continue clapping steadily)

"   "Like What, James?"
      (clap)   (clap)   (clap)   (clap)
      (clap)   (clap)   (clap)   (clap)

(James)   "Like the green stones in a ring."
      (clap) (clap) (clap) (clap)
      (clap) (clap) (clap) (clap)

4. Remind child to choose the next color:

(teacher)   "Your turn, James"
(James)   "I'm thinking of a color   and it
      (clap)   (clap)   (clap)   (clap)

"   is blue
      (clap)   (clap)   (clap)   (clap)

5. Ask "James" to choose another child to continue.

(James)   "Tanya!"
(Tanya)   "I'm thinking of a color   and it
      (clap)   (clap)   (clap)   (clap)

"   is blue
      (clap)   (clap)   (clap)   (clap)

"   like the cap on Jeffrey's head!"
      (clap)   (clap)   (clap)   (clap)

6. This child chooses another child and exercise continues as before. . .

(Tanya)	"I'm thinking of a color		and it	
	(clap)	(clap)	(clap)	(clap)
"	is yellow			
	(clap)	(clap)	(clap)	(clap)
"	"Heather!"			

After doing this exercise one time with your class, all you'll have to do is begin clapping four steady beats and the class will join in. Teachers tell me they've used this clapping exercise in many circumstances (lunchroom, field trips, etc.) when they wish to help a tired or noisy class regain its focus. "Clapping Colors" clears the intellectual palate, like sherbet that is served between courses of a strenuous meal.

Portraits

"Portraits" is not only a fun activity, but encourages the use of science vocabularies when studying the human body. The basic setup is simple:

My _____is like _____

_____

My _____are like _____

_____

My _____is like _____

_____

My _____are _____

_____ etc.

I live in _____

and eat _____

Encourage students to write as many similes as they like to describe themselves. With younger students, especially, it's a good idea to add an extra blank line after each line you write—for their details. Otherwise they're likely to write one-word similes. Also, notice how similes subtly shift into metaphors by simply dropping the 'like' in your poem model.

With first and second graders I might confine this exercise to their faces, being sure to add "accessories" such as freckles and braces and hairbands and earrings as "like what" possibilities.

It's a good idea to brainstorm lists of the areas of the body you wish students to concentrate on in their writing. For example, if you are studying the skeletal system, you might wish to make a list of solely skeletal parts; or, if you are studying the internal organs, you might wish your list to include kidneys, heart, lungs, etc.

You also may want to telescope your class's explorations to include all the parts of a hand (nails, metatarsals, knuckles, etc.), or the circulatory system (plasma, corpuscles, veins, arteries, etc.).

An interesting variation of self-portraits is family portraits, where a child chooses a family member as his or her subject, and using the same model as for self-portraits, describes the person's qualities using similes

> **You can reinforce subject-verb agreement with younger students by stressing how the verbs "is" and "are" must change in order to agree with either a singular or plural subject.**

and details. I usually encourage a wide range of choices for this exercise ranging from "Dad Portraits" and "Mom Portraits" to a portrait of one of the family pets. Don't be surprised if someone in your class sneaks in a teacher portrait for your scrutiny.

MY BODY

My hair is like a guzillion
skinny worms that are dead from
being dry. My eyes are like minny snowballs.
My ears are like tornadoes picking up dirt.
My nose is like two small tunnels with no way
out.
My teeth are like icicles hanging from a window.
My fingers are like Medusa's hair
waiting for someone to turn into stone.
I live in a T.V. and eat
the shows I don't like.

— Billie Davies, Grade 2

ME

My hair is like a forest with trees
falling down.
By bones are like little baseball
bats using my heart as the ball.
My eyes are like bird eggs with baby
birds still inside.
My nose is like a piece of wood
with two holes drilled into it.
My heart holds friendship that sends out
special greetings.
I live in Mrs. Giamo's brain and
eat all her ideas and homework assignments.

— John Sorriento, Grade 3

My hair is like spaghetti
    being painted in black ink;
My heart is like a pumper
    that never rests;
My eyes are like the sun
    that has been crashed into my skin;
My ears are like a tornado
    that has been spinning
        for years in my head. . .
. . . .
. . . .

— Jun Sun, Grade 3

My hair is like a mother snake
    searching for a place
      to have her baby;
. . . .
. . . .
My fingernails are like the twilight sky
    when I'm looking out the window;
. . . .
. . . .
My knuckle is like the universe
    spinning around and around.
      — Trissa Therien, Grade 3

My head is a place
    where dreams are kept;
My dreams are like icicles
    creeping along my roof.
I live in a rose
    and eat the silky, smooth petals.
      — Kate Slotwinski, Grade 3

My ears are like little gold mines
and people have heard I have
a top secret treasure and they
are looking for it. My brain
is like a pink T.V. that gives
me answers. I live in the earth
and eat up pollution and bad things
like bad bugs.
      — Chris Hart, Grade 2

MY HAIR

My hair is like a mushroom, a big, brown mushroom
that lives in a field high up.
My eyes are hazel and my eyes are like
cameras that watch everyone.
My fingers look like little tadpoles and
my fingernails look like the head of a tadpole.
My heart holds anger that's red.
I live in a dungeon and
eat earwax every morning for breakfast.
      — Billy Parke, Grade 5

"If" Poems

"IF" poems are great fun and their whole language possibilities are endless. But what I like most about them is their adaptability to almost any on-the-spot situation. I usually begin this activity by reading one of my own "If" poems:

BEING A KITE

If I were a kite
I'd kneel,
stretch my skinny arms
out wide,
and wait for wind.

My yellow shirt would
fill up like a sail
and flap,
tugging my criss-crossed
wooden bones and me
towards seas of cloud.

My rippling paper skin
would rustle like applause
as I inhaled,
gulping one last gust
to swoop me giddy-quick
above the trees.

My red rag tail
would drift
toward everything green
to balance me

so all day
   I could
      loop and climb
  loop and climb
     and
      soar
into pure sky.

— *Jacqueline Sweeney*

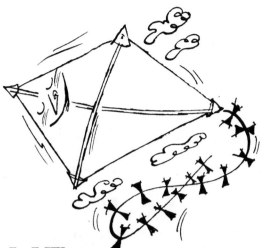

IF I WERE:

Put the following model on the blackboard:

> If I were a _____
> I'd _____
>   action
> I'd _____ and
>   action
> _____ etc.
>   action

You can ask for as many details as grade level and/or time will permit. Once you've presented the poem model, the "If I were . . . " variations are endless. Some possible topics include things, animals, and habitats.

THINGS:

> If I were a _____

computer	desk
radio	teacher
toaster	math quiz
planet	poster
telephone	coffeepot
globe	book
pencil	

Any of the above topics are suggested for use with the model, for example:

> If I were a toaster
> I'd heat up like a brainstorm.
> My mind would pop ideas up
> like golden toast.
> I'd have _____ etc.

If your children get stuck, refer them to the "Like What" list.

ANIMALS:

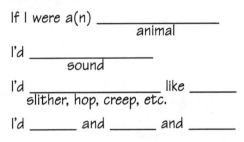

> If I were a(n) _____
>   animal
> I'd _____
>   sound
> I'd _____ like _____
>   slither, hop, creep, etc.
> I'd _____ and _____ and _____

HABITATS:

> If I were a _____
>   desert, ocean, rainforest, etc.
> I'd be_____
> I'd have_____
> I'd _____

After your children have fulfilled the requirements of a specific poem model in a written effort of their own, I think it's important to allow them to experiment. For example, they might wish to combine elements of one subject area with those of another—as I have combined elements of color, things, earth and nature in the following poem of mine:

CHOOSE A COLOR

If I were brown I'd be cattail
or turtle deep burrowed
in mud.

If I were orange
I'd be a newt's belly,

If yellow a willow
in Fall.

If pink I'd be a flamingo
or salmon
leaping upstream.

If I were blue
I'd be glacier,

If purple a larkspur
in Spring.

If I were silver
I'm sure I'd be river
  moonshattered
in liquid surprise.

If I were green
I'd be rainforest,

tree canopied.

If green I would help
the world

breathe.

— Jacqueline Sweeney

Models may vary greatly according to your design to include the specific qualities you wish to concentrate on with your students. I often circle on the "Like What" List the qualities I feel are most relevant to a particular subject—then ask students to choose any other qualities they feel work best for them.

Read some of the following children's sample poems to provide still more ideas for your class. I've included as wide a variety as possible here for you to choose from.

IF I WERE A FLUTE

I would play musical notes.
I would be silver sparkling stars.
I would have warm hands pressing on
my keys.
The air blowing through would warm
me all over.
When I'm in my case I should just be
waiting to get out and be played for
hours and hours everyday.
It makes me feel like the most
musical flute in the world.

— Amanda da Silva, Grade 5

THE WORLD

If I were the world
I'd turn and turn
I'd move around the sun
and my head would be the
world. My rippling skin would
be all ocean and would
stretch up like the waves
My clothes would be the
ragged land and get worn out
from the war, like clothes
getting washed 40 times.

— Jaclyn Gomez, Grade 5

IF I WERE A PENCIL SHARPENER

If I were a pencil sharpener,
I would tear off the pencil's skin.
I would be red like a berry.
I would taste like worms.
When my belly got full of pencil skins,
I'd take my head off
and throw them out.
I would feel like a balloon.
I would be the happiest thing
in the world.

— Aimee James, Grade 4

IF I WERE A RAINFOREST

If I were a rainforest
I'd stay still all day.
I'd be sticky and humid.
My hair would be long skinny vines that
animals swing from.
My arms would be branches of trees.
If I were a rainforest.

— Maria Schmitt., Grade 5

THE BLACK BEE

If I were a black bee
I'd buzz around town

I'd plump in a ball
My ears would be wings
My hair would be a
stinger

I'd soar like a bird above
the whole world.

My yellow swirls would
become stripes over my
spandex shirt

I'd soar through the sky
in yellow & black

I'd drop on someone
and stick in my stinger
        and fall to the ground.
        — Nicole DePompeis, Grade 5

If I were a flag hanging outside
I would sway back
and forth on a
pole. My hands would
be the stripes and my
hair would be the material.
I would be red, white and
blue. I would hang down
facing the ground
wondering if I
would ever hang
straight.
All day I would wish if
I could be like
the birds who fly
through the air and
I would be free.
        — Melissa Suter, Grade 5

If I were a president
I'd make rules
I'd make peace
and try to keep out of war.
I'd feel important.
My arms would GROW!
like grass on the lawn
My entire body would GROW tall!
My house will transform
like a leaf from season
to season.
The environment would change.
I would be in charge!
        — Jeff Renwick, Grade 5

A BIRD

Whenever I see a bird at mid-
day I get a strange feeling in my
head. So I go next door and act
like a bird flying over the fence,
and I swoop over a cat and it
jumps and leaps but it can't
catch me!
        — Richard DiStefano, Grade 3

IF PEOPLE WERE:

Another way to use the "If" format is to shift the focus from the persona of the writer to someone else. This shift allows for a more objective kind of observation—particularizing (more or less) as the teacher or student desires. For example, you might choose to have your students concentrate on people as a collective:

If people were weather
their hair would be clouds.
Their breath would be great winds.
Their _____ would be _____ etc.

or more particularized:

If people were buildings
Uncle Zack would be a skyscraper
with steel girders for bones
and big windows for eyes.

But mom would be a teepee
in a field of goldenrod
with deer skin flaps for
her soft ears and the
smoke of a cookie baking fire
swirling upward towards
the stars.

I suggest the following procedure:

1. Pick a topic for comparison (weather, buildings, trees)

2. Brainstorm parts of the chosen topic

3. Compare each part to its human counterpart

Suppose you decide to have your class write "If People Were Buildings" poems. First brainstorm a list similar to the following:

schools	factories
museums	igloos
pyramids	ranches
caves	police stations
tents	offices
churches	banks
greenhouses	firehouses
towers	skyscrapers
barns	arenas
warehouses	trailers
doghouses	birdhouses
treehouses	yachts
Twin Towers	The Capitol
Empire State Building	Washington Monument

Next choose one of the buildings and compare its parts to its human counterpart; for example: A SCHOOL. (Trust me, your students will come up with better ideas than you—at least they do this with me!—so it's best to brainstorm this part of the exercise with your children, also):

CAFETERIA = STOMACH
DOORS = MOUTH
ATTIC = HEAD
CLASSROOM = BRAIN
PRINCIPAL'S OFFICE = HEART
GYM = LEGS
LIBRARY = VEINS etc.

When this process is completed, offer a model or two:

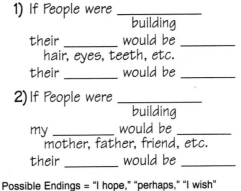

1) If People were _____
   building
   their _____ would be _____
   hair, eyes, teeth, etc.
   their _____ would be _____

2) If People were _____
   building
   my _____ would be _____
   mother, father, friend, etc.
   their _____ would be _____

Possible Endings = "I hope," "perhaps," "I wish"

If people were buildings,
my sister would be a birdhouse.
The post that holds up the birdhouse,
would be her long legs & small body.
The poles that stick out of the post,
and hold the food would be her arms & hands.
Her blood would be the bugs running through her
arms & legs.
Her head would be the house at
the top.
Her mouth would be the door that doesn't shut.
The windows would be her eyes.
Her nose would be the stick for the birds
to sit on.
Her heart would provide the warmth for the birds.
Perhaps, someday this will come true.
— Laura Lynn, Grade 5

If people were buildings my mom
would be a restaurant.
The windows would be teeth.
The kitchen would be her hands.
The food would be her stomach.
Her nose hairs would be the spaghetti
cooking in a pot.
Her nose would be an olive that is
waiting to be eaten.
Her mouth would be a sliced tomato.
I wish I could be a restaurant too!
— Christelle Munnelly, Grade 5

If People were a hockey rink
Their smooth bald head would be
the cold clear ice.
The pucks would be the teeth
falling out into the crowd.
The voice would be the cheering
of the crowd.
Their ears would be the sticks
of two people checking each other.
The nose would be the ticket booth
because the person says: "Pick
your seat." Perhaps I will be one.
— Tyler Johnson, Grade 5

PEOPLE AS TRAILERS

If people were like trailers
their stomach would be the kitchen where
all the food is.
Their car would be legs that would
bring them places.
their hair would be trees that
swayed with the wind.
Their room would be a head that
held all their knowledge.
Their bed would be the mouth without
teeth.
Maybe we could be trailers for
just one day, but go back to ourselves
at night.

— Rebecca Commerford, Grade 5

If People were a cave
their mouth would be the closing
their eyes would be the opening
in the cave that brings in light
their hair would be the water
dripping down from the ceiling
their skin would be the outside
which is beautiful but their
heart sould be the dark inside made of stone.
Some people are probably already
caves.

— Sarah Delena, Grade 5

If people were buildings
I would definitely say, my friend Evan
would be like a house. His hair is
straight like the shingles on the roof.
His skin would be the wood that is
waterproof. His breath would be the smoke
from the fireplace. But of course
his face would be the door welcoming you in
to stay for the day. His heart is in
the 2nd floor.

— Vincent Galvin, Grade 5

You might take liberties with opening lines, as the following poem of mine suggests:

FAMILY TREES

People are like
walking trees
with sweatered limbs
and fingered leaves.

I'll bet they shop
at oak boutiques
and willow
haberdasheries.

Some folks wear suits
of fitted tweed
with acorn buttons
on each sleeve,

while some wear capes
flamboyant green
that flap and twirl
with every breeze.

I've seen a swirling
people-tree
conduct a stormy
symphony!

The roots of trees
grow underground,
but rooted folks
must walk around;

most people-roots
have heels and toes,
and where they walk
the whole tree goes.

So if you pass a
walking tree
with shoelace vines
and fingered leaves,

be sure to smile
and be polite.
It just might be
your family.

— Jacqueline Sweeney

As you can see, the format variations for this activity are endless. You can construct "If People Were . . ." poems not only about weather, buildings and trees, but also about plants, fish, furry animals, vehicles, furniture, etc. I've only shown you the entire writing process for "If People Were Buildings," otherwise this section would never end. I would like to close "If People Were . . ." with one more poem by Andrew Murphy, because I think he does me one better when it comes to entering the realm of feeling and magic— which I asked for!

IF PEOPLE WERE TREES

If people were trees
their ears are
like the holes where owls
stay. Their hair is like
leaves that sway.
Their skin is like the rough
frail bark. Their hearts are like
the flowers that blossom with
unconditional love.
— Andrew Murphy, Grade 5

IF MY FACE WERE OUTER SPACE:

This is a fun way for students to review their outer space vocabularies, because they must explore each word's qualities before comparing it to the appropriate facial counterpart.

I suggest you begin with a list of current outer space vocabulary words, such as the phases of star development, names of planets, etc. Include whatever is helpful to your classroom focus at the moment.

Next provide a list of pertinent outer space adjectives. As always, word lists come quickest when brainstormed with the class.

pocked	streaking	swirling
shining	pale	bubbling
burning	whirling	luminous
twinkling	sparkling	frozen
round	roaring	shooting
icy	orbiting	bright
revolving		etc.

If time is a factor, simply reading the following poem will be enough to stimulate thinking, and the brainstorming can be left to the individual child. Each activity allows for flexibility of schedules and the amount of preparation you wish to do before asking your students to write.

IF MY FACE WERE OUTER SPACE
My eyes would be bright moons
glowing green or brown or blue;
my cheeks would be round mountain
slopes on Mars.

My nostrils would be craters;
my pores would be dwarf stars.
I'd make eyebrow explorations
in small solar powered cars.

My mouth would be a black hole
searching endlessly for food;
sucking up space objects
like a vacuum cave of doom.

I'd have galaxies of freckles,
and soaring asteroid moles,
and spinning satellite pimples
orbiting my nose.

My dimples would be channels
leading to my lips and chin
and the smoothest curve of Venus
where my smiles all begin.

My hair would be like Saturn's
rings reflecting heat and light;
swirling 'round my head until
I go to bed at night.

I'd have rotating stations
floating upright as my ears
listening in on conversations
that I'm not supposed to hear;

and I'd listen in
for years and years
and years and years
and years!

— Jacqueline Sweeney

If my face were outer space
my hair would be the Milky Way
My nose would be the sun
that shines
throughout my
face
My eyes would
be great planets
of the Green sparkling Uranus
and Neptune
My pores would be
craters and my
skin lunar soil
My mouth would be
the dark Black Hole
out of nowhere
My freckles would
be the great constellations
of Lew, Pegasus, Hercules, Little
dipper, and the Big Dipper
and my dimple would
be the bright shining
Star
It makes me feel
free and on top of the world
but it makes me feel lonely
because there is no life
that stops, they keep pass-
ing on never ever stop,
they are gone.
— Sarah Delena, Grade 5

IF MY FACE WERE OUTER SPACE
If my face
were outer space
my hair
would be
The Sea of Tranquility
very gray and still . . .
My nose would
be a spacecraft
exploring
the lunar surface
My mouth would
be the asteroid belt
with many many
asteroids
My whole
head would be
the moon
boring and dull
My eyelashes
would be dust and spots
in space
always moving
My eyes
would be
Saturn and Jupiter
with many,
many, many
many colored rings
always rotating
— Paul Plekon, Grade 5

If my face were outerspace
my eyes would be craters on Mars.
Mars would be my face with shooting
stars and comets circling around,
my mouth would be the Sea of
Tranquility, inside it would be dark as
the black hole sucking in meteors for
food and drinking the Milky Way, and
every time I burped
earth would have a tornado.
— Kris McGowan, Grade 5

If my face were outerspace
my eyes would be The Black Hole.
My nose would be the spout in the
Milky Way. My tears when I'm
sad would be shooting stars.
When I get mad I shoot meteorites.
I change my face by the planets.
If I get mad I change to Mars.
If I get cool I change to Neptune.
When I get lips like Jupiter
I get craters. Yes, I like my face
because it's outer space.
— Kyra Johnston, Grade 5

If my face were outer space
my eyes would be round like
a planet. My mouth would sound like
an asteroid hitting the Earth.
My teeth would be cold
like Pluto. My dry throat
would be like the Sea of
Tranquility. It would make me
feel large.
— Tommy Miller, Grade 5

If my face were outer space
my face would be the planet
Uranus with my glasses as its
white moons swirling around
my face.
     My mouth would be
the Black Hole sucking up
everything in sight like a
vacuum sucking up dirty dirt.
     My eyes would be bright
stars lighting up space like
two lamps turned on forever
— Sarah Sairitupa, Grade 5

Art Adventures

MUSIC POEMS:

Music poems are quick and easy and the perfect "plug in" exercise to calm a rowdy class before lunch, after lunch, or prior to dismissal.

1. Choose a piece of music you like—one that is instrumental.

2. Ask the children to close their eyes and try to see pictures or a story in their minds as you play the selection.

3. Refer them to the "Like What" List as a point of reference, then play the musical selection again; this time asking your children to write their impressions as they are listening. Have them concentrate on sounds—colors—smells. Do they visualize a scene? Ask them to let their minds float along and give their imaginations free rein. Explain that their pictures may change suddenly —and that's okay.

4. While playing the selection a third time, if necessary, have the children write their impressions.

5. Share the results.

Suggested Music:

My personal favorite is Moussorgsky's PICTURES AT AN EXHIBITION, because the composer has written twelve short, complete pieces of music—each one his own musical impression—of paintings from an art exhibit he saw in his native country, Russia.

I especially like Moussorgsky's "Ballet of the Unhatched Chicks" because it's a lot like the music children encounter as accompaniments to cartoons. "Bydlo," on the other hand, suggests the movement of an ox slowly pulling a cart up a hill, over the crest, and down the other side. "The Great Gate of Kiev" is full of majesty with lots of crashing cymbals and thundering kettle drums.

Other musical selections I've used successfully in classrooms include Stravinsky's "Rite of Spring" (don't feel compelled to use the entire piece!) and Kodály's "Háry János Suite," which is the musical retelling of a Hungarian folk tale. I like it because the music is exhilarating and accessible to children, and because it's broken down into sections, e.g., "The Viennese Musical Clock"—each one like a small chapter in a book. I've used this piece as an entire lesson where the children follow the actual story in their minds as they hear its musical counterpart.

> **Don't tell the children what the music is about until *after* they've written their own impressions.**

Sometimes I play selections from "Song of the Humpbacked Whale," which is an album devoted entirely to the wonderful communications of these creatures (without musical accompaniment of any kind!). As I play each of the diverse sounds of the whales, I don't tell the children what the subject is; I simply ask them to write their feelings and impressions with each one. Afterwards, I explain the real source of the "ocean music" they've just heard.

Don't hesitate to use any musical selection that appeals to you: Blues, Jazz, "The Flight of the Bumblebee," Bach, Mozart, etc. All music inspires its own colors, mood, and imagery.

CHILDREN'S SAMPLE POEMS:

After hearing "Ballet of the Unhatched Chicks" by Moussorgsky:

I see some little people like me.
I hear some people talk like me.
I feel like singing out—
"I like you. I like you."
— *Benjamin Jenkins, Grade 2*

I saw a big hawk.
It feels like he's going to
kill someone.
The music tastes like paint.
The music feels wet.
This tune makes me feel happy.
I saw the color green.
The big hawk flew over
all the houses.
— *Chris Wilson, Grade 1*

Like when people get mad and their
faces get red. Sounds like
the people chomping watermelon.
They're in such a hurry they fall
with their faces smushed in cakes.
It smells like someone cooking good
food. Tastes as good as Jello cake.
— *Rinah Davis, Grade 1*

I see spots all around me.
I see spots, flying, moving
circling around.
I'm in another world.
Dizzy— red, blue, green
all around.
— *Terrence Brooks, Grade 3*

After hearing Moussorgsky"s "Bydlo":

I saw a Pegasus leap and spring
over a rainbow and spread his
graceful white wings to show he
was master. And then it started
to lightening and thunder, and he
came down to earth and gave it a
mighty stamp with his powerful hoof
and all the animals in creation hailed him
forever after!
— *Kim Kelly, Grade 4*

After hearing "Divertimento for String Orchestra: Finale Furioso" by Bela Bartok:

I feel very scared because somebody
is chasing me.
I smell something bad.
I see my mom and dad and I want to
go home.
— *Frank Richardson, Grade 1*

After hearing Whale Sounds:

It sounded like a werewolf
on a hill and having blood
dripping.
It felt scared.
It sounded like a walrus
trying to get up.
And it was calling me.
It sounds like the ocean.
It sounds like a giant black mon-
ster taking a bath.
It sounds like a haunted city
with a hole in the middle.
— Asheda Walker, Grade 2

After hearing "The Nutcracker":

There's a lonely queen,
    a lovely queen
        like
      the sun,
        moon,
in a yellow
      and
        blue sadness.
Hey, the queen
    with her beautiful
        dancers,
her lovely dancers
    look like
        a
    rainbow
spinning over my head
    like
happiness sailing
    across
the ocean.
— Helen Monge, Grade 5

THE NUTCRACKER AND ME
It was like being in a dark,
red room
with hearts pumping
    around me.
It felt like being
    in another world.
It made me feel like
    being on the moon.
It was like being
    in the wilderness
    with the leaves dancing
    next to me
      and
Rocks jumping
    up and down.
— Paul Deeny, Grade 5

PAINTING POEMS:

This activity provides children the opportunity to explore character, setting, color, and mood through visual art. The format will more than likely assume the shape of a story, but this is okay.

I suggest you show your class a painting that you yourself are drawn to—for whatever reason. Your choice need not be an elaborately framed original. It could be a print from your home, one on loan from the library, or one from a book. I find that portraits work very well as do paintings that create dramatic impact. Once you've chosen a painting, the rest is easy, for the colors and context and story of the painting will do the rest to inspire your class.

1. Present your chosen painting to the class, being sure to give them plenty of time to look at it quietly before you offer any directions.

2. Ask your students to imagine they are a character in the painting.

3. Ask them to close their eyes and imagine what the character is feeling and thinking.

4. Ask them to notice the dominant colors and allow these colors to drift through their bodies—making them feel hot or cold, lonely or excited or angry, etc.

5. Next ask your children to think of themselves as the character, and consider:

- who they are
- how they got there
- what their title or occupation is
- what they're feeling?
- why they're feeling that way?
- their plans for the future
- whether they are rich or poor

6. You may wish to ask a few questions and brainstorm some responses with your class to prompt detailed thinking:

- Do people like them (as the character)?
- Are they kind or mean to others?
- Do they have a family? etc.

7. Put the following model on the board to stimulate thinking:

I'm a _____

My eyes will tell you that I'm _____

lonely, peaceful, etc.

I'm wearing a _____

that_____

drapes around me, etc.

like _____

I come from _____

where I _____

8. Ask your children to use only the parts of the model

that work for their poems and their particular meanings, being sure to encourage those who are inclined to create their own poems in their own styles.

Here are some optional lines I've used to keep the poem (and thinking) moving:

A. Behind me/Beside me is a _____ which I use for _____
B. Sometimes I like to _____
C. I long for the days when _____
D. I look forward to _____
E. I wish _____

There are so many wonderful paintings ranging from Medieval times to the present, I suggest you simply get an illustrated history of art and choose something that you like. An alternative is to begin with a collection of nineteenth and twentieth century art and work your way back. I'll list a few artists and paintings below that I have used; but understand, it's a meager list and leaves out many fine artists.

Degas	"Cafe Singer"
	"Laundress"
Winslow Homer	"The Gulf Stream"
Picasso	"Pierrot"

as well as many portraits by Mary Cassatt and Henri de Toulouse-Lautrec.

You might select several paintings, divide your class into groups, and have each individual in the group present his/her written impression of the selected painting. This way, when you share your class's written results, you are not only sharing multiple points of view about each work of art, but enabling your class to experience several paintings in the same time span they would otherwise experience only one.

Other artists I've used:

Botticelli	Van Gogh
Dürer	Gaugin
Rembrandt	Gustave Klimt
El Greco	Matisse
Michelangelo	Monet
Leonardo	Holbein
	and many, many more.

Textures

WORD TEXTURES:

Every word has a texture. To me, the word "finesse" feels smooth as lavender silk. As an expanded image, "finesse" would feel smooth as the lavender silk dress my aunt wore on her twenty-fifth wedding anniversary.

The word "ratchet" might feel sharp as porcupine quills or rough as the bark of the black walnut tree I climbed as a child.

To explore word textures with your class, first choose a word. You might wish to peruse the dictionary for a quick list, because it should be a word with which your students are unfamiliar.

Ask your children to close their eyes and say the word silently to themselves. Is it soft? Hard? Smooth? Bumpy? Slimy?

Brainstorm the word's qualities together as a class. You might wish to have certain students write the word's qualities as they'd appear in Nature, while other students write the word's qualities in weather, and still others write the word's qualities in clothing imagery, or food imagery.

Words I've used:

ligature	snaffle
chuckwala	mollify
snick	arachnoid
flotsam	gigolo
pretentious	flannelette
glut	attribute
mitzvah	pasha
pizzicato	grackle
chronicle	accelerando
sluice	churlish
sesame	

NAME POEMS:

This activity is an extension of the texture exercise and is quite versatile because the children can write about their own names, the names of people in their families—or you can assign a name or name grouping from which to choose. For example, your class might be studying early American history; therefore you might wish to make a list of some popular early American names:

Ethan	Ezechial
Edith	Rebecca
Benjamin	Jeremiah
Anne	Sarah
Virginia, etc.	

Some other groupings might include:

Mythological	Native American
Astronauts	Explorers
Frontiersmen	Presidents
Inventors	Painters
Musicians	
Battles (Civil War or Revolutionary War)	

You might assign a name to each child from a group that you are studying currently, or have each child draw a name from a hat.

When writing about names of historical figures ask students to try to incorporate some of the individual's qualities into the poem's language and imagery. If you have time, you might brainstorm a list of appearance as well as character traits. For instance:

<u>Tecumseh:</u>

dark	strong	swift
powerful	stocky	agile

wrestler	fearless	leader
horseman	brother	bowman
crafty	kind	fair
warrior		

<u>When it's time to write:</u>

1. Put the following list on the board for reference:
   - weather
   - clothing
   - a texture
   - food
   - a thing
   - a quality
   - something in nature

2. Ask the children to choose any *four* from the above list to use in the following model:

_____ is _____ (like) optional
Name   adjective
    It is _____
    It is _____
    It is _____
    It is _____
(ending) It is _____
    quality or makes me feel...

Note: You may substitute "he" or "she" for 'it.'

Sample:

Lucinda is curious.
She is the cat at the window;
the mystery book on the
library shelf.
She's yellow earmuffs.
She's a lemon drop
and warm spring rain.
Lucinda is ____ (strong, vivacious, etc.)
    quality

Carl is swirly.

He is the ocean
lapping rocks.

He is a tall tale
on a windy night.

He is mud boots and
leather gloves.

He is broccoli and
boiled carrots.

Carl is _____ (strong, wild, etc.)

ALEXANDER THE GREAT

Alexander, you are like a gold
lightening bolt.
Alexander, you have steel arms for
arms and legs.
I am envious toward you, Alexander.
You have the strongness of an
ox pulling a cart.
You are a vicious night in winter
You grab me into your time
When you conquered the world, a place
Where I can wonder about life as it was.
When you ran the world like
it was a little yellow flower that
makes me feel powerless like I'm
an ant in a giant's world.
— Sarah Winner, Grade 6

GEORGE WASHINGTON

George Washington is
like a white blossom.
It's like a blue stream
flowing from the mountain
like a silver dollar.
It makes me feel cold
when I walk through
the snow.
It makes me feel
dead when he fires the
guns.
— James Ridgway, Grade 4

Richard is strong like steel.
He is the shape of a spoon.
His name is crunchy
like a dog chewing on a bone.
Richard is the color of a gold ring.
I like that name because it is my
dad's name.
— Matthew Kline, Grade 4

GENEVA

Geneva makes me feel like autumn.
She is like a delicate flower.
This is my grandmother's name.
When she works, she works like a
young girl enjoying herself.
It reminds me of hopping.
And playing.
She soars around the house while
she works.
— Erika Nelson, Grade 3

Just For Fun

FILL IN THE FISH:

This is a nonsense activity based on one of my poems, and I suggest you play it for laughs. The format lends itself to many fish variations, but my favorites are goldfish, guppy, minnow, etc. because the concept is so ridiculous.

A FISH IN SCHOOL

A man-eating

_____
                   goldfish, guppy, etc.
was 'round here today.
A man-eating _____
was looking for prey.
It swam past the windows.
It swam past the doors.
It swam in huge circles
all over the floor.
It swallowed _____'s sneakers.
           child's name
It swallowed _____'s hat.
           child's name
It swallowed the _____'s
                janitor, principal, etc.
striped orange cat.
Now what does a fish-eating kid
think of that?
Here's what I think of that . . .
  (repeat poem with new fish)
        — Jacqueline Sweeney

Either you call out the name of the next fish or animal, or call on a child in your class to choose one, and chant the poem again.

If I ask the children to write this exercise, I simply circle the words: man-eating prey swam fish-eating and ask them to change the circled words to suit their own meanings in poems of their own.

Some suggested topic variations:
- a coat-eating zebra
- a sock-eating cobra
- a book-eating sand flea
- a wall-swallowing wallaby, etc.

The only requirement for this activity is a longing for fun and the willingness to be absurd!

TREASURE HUNT:

This is an exercise in logic and imagery and can be as simple or complex as you desire.

1. Hide an object or objects in your classroom (or wherever!) while the class is absent from the premises.

2. Have your class try to guess where the object is after each clue.

For example, you might hide a new eraser and the one who guesses the hiding place gets to keep it.

Sample:

"It's inside a monster
that's metal and wood.   (clue #1)

It's big mouth is dark
as a cave.   (clue #2)

It devours old homework
and pencils and books." etc. (clue #3)

(answer: a desk)

"It's tucked between old trees
now flattened and white.   (clue #1)

Blue icicles streak
left and right.   (clue #2)

It sometimes gets crumpled
like snowballs in flight,   (clue #3)

soaring its way to the
green classroom floor;   (clue #4)

never a trashcan
in sight!"

(answer: notebook paper)

You can divide your class into teams that create their own treasure hunt clues. Then have each team present its clues one by one, and ask the rest of the class to guess the whereabouts of each others' hidden treasures.

It's sometimes a good idea to set guidelines for clues: a maximum or minimum number, each clue must have a simile—or one color and one texture—or one shape, etc.

"Treasure Hunt" is especially useful before holidays involving the exchange of gifts or as part of the class's celebration of a student's birthday.

CONCRETE MATH:

Choose a number and look at it with your class. Does it look like something besides a number? Turn the number on its side. What does it resemble now?

The number "8", for example, might look like a pair of glasses when put on its side, while the number 1,000.000 resembles a train—with the zeros forming the wheels, or maybe the cars of the train.

As you brainstorm together, ask your children to think about the power of certain numbers—how the simple placement of the number "1" to the left or right of another number can drastically alter its value.

Next ask if an addition, subtraction, or long division formation changes the look of certain numbers. What about fractions?

Ask your students to each choose a number. Prompt them with questions as they're choosing: Is it your favorite? Why? Is it the number on a mailbox or a football shirt? Does it bring luck?

Next ask each child to write the chosen number at the top of a piece of paper (unlined paper works best), then say:

(look at) 1. "Look at the number. Twist it around. Turn it on its side. Look again. Use your imagination and write all the things your number resembles.

(action) 2. Does it do anything special in your imagination such as dance across the page, or hopscotch, or slither like a snake?

(feeling) 3. Tell how you feel about your number."

Here is a model you might wish to put on the board:

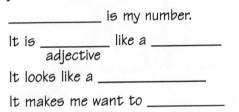

_____ is my number.

It is _____ like a _____
        adjective

It looks like a _____

It makes me want to _____

Some lines I've offered classes to keep the poem moving:

1. On its side it turns into a _____
2. Upside down it is _____
3. Add _____ to my number and it _____
4. I _____ number
       feeling
We first met _____
  at the mailbox, on the baseball field, etc.

TWO

Two makes me happy.
Two twirls and twirls
like a line making turns.
Two is bright red
like a male cardinal's feathers.
Two is not sloppy,
Two is neat.
Two is always near.
Two is a friend.
Two makes me feel like I'm liked.
— Holly Weidenbacher, Grade 5

88 THE WORSE

88 makes me feel old
just like my father and mother.
88 are two pairs of glasses
and four eyes.
88 is gold like the
stars at night.
— Christopher Latka, Grade 3

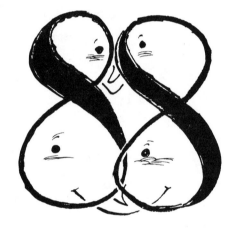

ZERO

O is my number,
I wish I can be O,
Then I don't have to go to school,
O is like balls, doughnuts, tires,
and bowling balls.
— Jessica Horvath, Grade 2

THE NUMBER ONE

. . . It's plain and
just sits there like a
frog waiting for a fly.
In a way it's lucky. It's
always first no matter how
you look at it. Who ever
invented these numbers
including the number one
should have
dressed it up
somehow or
another. The
number 1 has
great power
for its size. It
can change
another number
just by putting
ONE little line
in front or
behind

O N E

— Laurie Ford, Grade 5

MATH

Math is
numbers of many
combos.
Adding
is a piece
of cake.
Subtraction
is a spicy
slice of
pizza.
Multiplication
is a muddy pie.
Division is Jello—
always shaky.
Algebra is the condemner,
and calculus the executioner.
— *Jessica Nolfo, Grade 7*

13 is my number. It just stands there gazing all around. If you put the number 13 together it becomes a 'B' in the alphabet. It floods the ocean's island. It looks like a nut in a peanut butter sandwich. The number 13 feels like a bubble in the air. And the soap in the sink. It sounds like a shriek like a step creaking. I feel light as a feather falling from the blue and white sky.
— *Naomi Lager, Grade 4*

NUMERAL

Numerals are numbers but more than numbers.
They can be used in Math, Algebra, or made
        to count cucumbers.
They tell you how old you are
        or how young you are.
I like numerals better than numbers
        because—
Numbers just spit out of a pen or pencil
But numerals are thoughts that jump out
        of your brain.
— *John Greet, Grade 8*

Weather

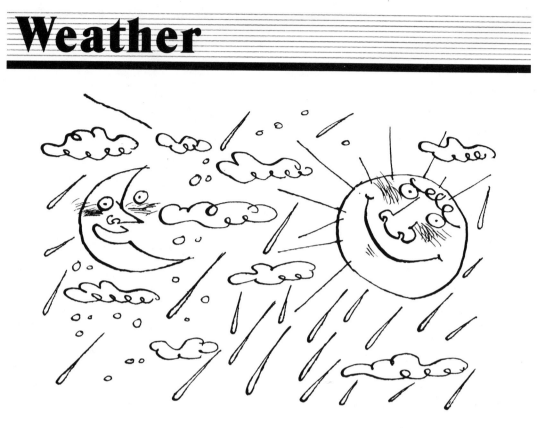

WEATHER CREATURE:

Weather is a theme that appears in every second through fifth grade classroom in one capacity or another, and although teachers continually express interest in "weather poems," they've also expressed how tired they are of hearing weather described with the same old cliches. After all, how many ways can you present themes of snow and rain or sunshine year after year without wilting from boredom? I created the activity "Weather Creature" for this reason and to put a little pizzazz into my own weather presentations. Now, after brainstorming the usual weather words for possible poem topics (sun, fog, snow, rain, hail, sleet, etc.), and referring children to the 'Like What' list, I add another option: "Weather Creature." Then I invite the class to put some *action* into its weather poems and try to write about weather in a new way.

1. When you brainstorm weather and weather-related words with your class, be sure to include the seasons and words like "freezing," "melting," "cold," "hot," etc.

2. Put some possible first lines on the board:

A. _____ is like _____
　　weather

B. When it _____
rains, is windy, is hot and sticky, etc.
the _____ _____ like _____
　　weather action

3. You might offer a few creative first lines of your own. For example:

A. "Rain is like a giant's tears . . .

B. "Snow looks like white feathers fluttering in moonlight . . ."

4. You might read a few weather poems you like to set the mood and present ideas to your students.

5. Read the following poem by Lilian Moore that transforms winter into a witch who controls weather conditions with strong verb commands:

DECEMBER 21
Old Witch Winter,
is riding high,
this day of her longest
night.

"Ice!"
she shrieks.
No puddle is safe,
roofs bristle with
spears.

"Light
begone!"
she whistles.
Dusk appears.

"Shiver!"
she snarls.
We heed, and
huddle in our
skins.

Thermometers
bleed to
zero,

but something new
begins.
　　　　　　　— Lilian Moore

6. Ask your children to look at the weather words on the board and consider transforming their choices of seasons or 'weather' into a creature full of action and/or commands.

7. Put the following model for a title on the board:

_____　　_____
weather/season　　creature

Some suggested titles:

AUTUMN PRINCESS　KING WINTER
QUEEN SPRING　　　SNOW BEAST
WATER WIZARD

8. Offer some first lines if necessary:

A. When the _____ _____ ____
　　　　　　weather creature action

　it _____

B. I am _____ _____

　I _____
　　　action
　I _____
　　　action

9. After reading the following children's sample poems, ask your students to choose their own topics and/or poem models from the board and write their own poems.

THE TERRIBLE THUNDER LIZARD

There is a tyrannosaurus in me.
It has sharp teeth like fangs on a snake.
It lives in my brain. It makes
me roar in my brain like
an elephant. It makes me
do bad things like I broke
my neighbor's window last week
with a snowball.
It can tear apart
the good side of my brain
and leave the bad side.
I wish it could not make
me do bad things.
— *Nick Bigelow, Grade 2*

STORM CREATURE

When the storm creature cries
it rains. When he spins a coin
a tornado builds up. Sunshine is
when he turns on the light.
Fog is when he coughs.
Wind is when he sneezes.
When he drips a glass of
water he makes a tidal wave.
When he drops water and it
hits a cord it makes thunder.
When he opens the freezer
it starts winter. Earthquake is
when he jumps. When he slops a
little water it drizzles. When
he opens his closet and everything falls an avalanche is made.
— *Justin Saglibene, Grade 4*

WHEN IT SNOWS

When it snows the tree tops
turn white and it looks like old
people. It sounds like it is
weeping and it's soft and it almost
makes me go to sleep.
— *Michelle Raulf, Grade 3*

A TREE IN WINTER

A tree in winter has icicles
hanging like golden fingers. And the
trunk is the size of a big snow beast
with ice for eyes. And he has an
icicle for a spear. IT IS VERY
SCARY TO LOOK AT A TREE
IN WINTER.
— *Chris Damiana, Grade 3*

FOG!

Fog like a hog
Fog takes up room
Move over I say!
         GO
                  AWAY!
— *Melissa Shields, Grade 4*

SUNSHINE PRINCESS

I am a sunshine princess.
When I see a storm I turn into
sunshine and it will never turn
into a storm.
I can turn ugly things into
sunshine. The sunshine princess
loves animals. She even
takes her dog with her.
— Jennifer Gibson, Grade 2

WHEN IT IS STICKY IN THE SUMMER

When it is sticky you are hot. Your clothes
stick to you. The sun is like it is in the
desert. It is sputtering. It is so hot
you sweat. Then suddenly it starts to rain.
The thunder pounds. Everybody is scared.
When I am afraid I hide under my covers
in the night. The lightening is like

a

crack

in

the

wall.
— Alana Descere, Grade 3

WHEN IT IS WINDY

When it is windy the grass
cries against the wind like
screeching children. The trees
sound like howling wind. The wind
rushing against the house is like
a screaming elephant. And then
it calms down. It is soft as
little kids whispering.
— Suzanne Potts, Grade 3

PRINCESS STORM

I am Princess Storm. When my
high-heels click it is the rain
pitter-pattering on the sidewalk.
My earrings flickering in the light
is the lightening. When I pound my
fists it is the roaring thunder
in the sky.
That's how I am,
that's me.
— Erica Finizio, Grade 4

CRAZY TITLES:

This exercise is quick and painless, and it is an excellent way to introduce describing words (adjectives) and reinforce the usage of nouns.

1. First put a selection of titles on the board—either borrowed from my samples below or created by you to relate more closely to the nouns and adjectives in:

   a. the current week's vocabulary list

   b. current themes in science, history, language arts, etc.

2. Next ask your students to choose one of the titles that interests them and make it the title of their poems.

3. Show your children how to brainstorm each word of the title separately. For example, break down a salad into its component parts in "Scary Salad"—then tell what each part stands for (radishes are red, beady eyes, lettuce is witch's hair, etc.).

4. Prompt with questions: Do the olives spit or scream at the approaching fork? Do the tomatoes sneer? Do the cucumbers cackle? What makes the salad scary?

5. Direct your students to the "Like What" List for reference and encourage them to tell a story.

6. Prior to your class beginning to write, read some sample poems by other children.

SOME SAMPLE "CRAZY TITLES":

Sad Sneakers	Screaming Shoes
Silver Eyes	Red Dreams
Hairy Worms	Silly Spaghetti
A Giant Fib	Mean Thorns
Dancing Fleas	Grumpy Sky
Singing Stars	Chocolate Trees
Sizzling Snakes	Hot Toes

For a more spontaneous generation of titles try creating word cans (I use coffee cans)—one filled with nouns, the other filled with adjectives. Write the nouns on one color paper and the adjectives on another color, so the children can easily visualize a distinction between the two parts of speech. Have the children draw one of each to create their own truly unpredictable titles.

CHILDREN'S SAMPLE POEMS:

PEACEFUL PENNIES

Peaceful pennies sound like fingers snapping when I drop them into a pond.

— Nicole Phelps, Grade 2

CRYING DREAMS

Crying dreams are like blue rain.
They dance in my dreams when I am asleep.

— Amy Beyor, Grade 2

Left Out Freckles are like baseball players that no one is talking to. Left Out Freckles are like dreams that have not been thought of yet. Left Out Freckles are like flags that are not being looked at. Left Out Freckles are like icicles not being licked. Left Out Freckles live on a face.
— Andrea Tonkin, Grade 2

GIANT FIBS

I told my mother I was going to slay
    a dragon
I really didn't.
I told my mother I was a magical
    princess
I really wasn't.
I told my mother I was a wicked
    witch and I was going to turn
    her into a frog
I really didn't.
I told my mother I saw a giant
I really didn't.
          — Nicole Satterwhite, Grade 4

WOBBLY FEELINGS
Strange wobbly feelings are like feelings that hide inside yourself. They just pound in your stomach. They never want to come out. It's just feelings that are sad.
— Chrissy George, Grade 5

WILD WORMS
Wild worms say bad words.
Wild worms eat people.
Wild worms live in JENland
They sound like bees
buzzing around a cow.
    — Jen Buckworth, Grade 3

Mystery Boxes

MYSTERY BOX:

Any time you bring a closed box into your classroom, your students will be intrigued. Simply listening to questions about the box's contents could take up those spare ten minutes before lunch. One of the most versatile "box" activities is "Mystery Box" and it should be just that—a box—filled with items the children might not be readily able to identify; for example, some locust shells, unusual seeds, a milkweed pod, a conglomerate rock, an apparatus from an electronic device, etc.

Place one of the objects on your desk, or better yet walk it around, allowing each child to look and touch. Next, ask the children to describe the object using "like whats." Now have them write about the object. Ask them to guess what it is used for. After you share their written conjectures and descriptions, tell them the object's real identity and function.

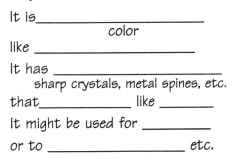

It is_____
                   color

like _____

It has _____
     sharp crystals, metal spines, etc.

that_____ like _____

It might be used for _____

or to _____ etc.

HEIRLOOM BOX:

This box should be filled with interesting items that either look or really are OLD: an old kaleidoscope, a garnet rosary, a leather-covered book with a date and inscription, someone's diary in another language, old jewelry and small jewelry boxes, stuffed toys, etc.

I begin this activity by explaining to the children that each item in the box was once owned by someone long ago—someone who loved it. Sometimes I tell them an item has had many owners, and if it could talk it would tell us an interesting story—sometimes sad, sometimes full of adventure.

I suggest you pass the items around to small groups, stressing that the children should hold each item and try to imagine:

WHO   owned it (a doctor in Texas? Queen Victoria?)

WHAT   is it?

WHERE   it lived (on a kitchen shelf in Cleveland?)

WHEN   it lived there (100 years ago? With the dinosaurs?)

You might find it helpful to ask the children to *become* the object and try to speak for it. For example:

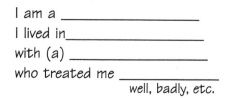

I am a _____
I lived in_____
with (a) _____
who treated me _____
                well, badly, etc.

You might ask the children (as their objects) if they have a sad or funny story to tell. I ask about their former owners and how they were treated and where they are now, and I often find with this exercise that I must continually prompt students with questions, or they will submerge themselves in the object's qualities and get lost.

To help children get started I usually pick out one or two of the objects and make up a story about it. For example, I might choose a stuffed, yellow calico horse with red yarn hair. I might tell the children I am the horse and speak for it. For example:

"I have hair like red fire
from a sunset and my fur
is like a yellow field of flowers.
I lived with a little girl named
Elly in the Old West. She took
me with her on a wagon train.
Every night I slept beside her—
and she hugged me as we traveled
over icy mountains and through
deep rivers. Later I lived with her
in a cabin her father built in the
wilderness. She loved me a lot and
gave me to her own little girl who
kept me on a shelf in her bedroom in
Kansas City. I wish . . . .etc."

You will, of course, be offering many more story details than the children will include in their story/poems about their "heirlooms"—but each child will take something different from the ideas you present and use it in his or her own way.

BOX OF MOMENTS AND DAYS:

I like to use an old cigar box for this exercise, but any box will do. You might even wish to design one with sparkles and colors and give it a prominent position in your classroom's Writing Center or Creative Corner— where your children can go to work on small writing projects in their spare time.

Once you've chosen an appropriate "box":

1. Cut out strips of colored paper (the more colors the better).

2. Upon each colored strip write one of the following phrases and mix them up in the box:

THE BEST DAY OF MY LIFE
MY MOST EXCITING TIME
MY WORST FEAR
MY SADDEST DAY
MY HAPPIEST MOMENT
MY CALMEST MOMENT
MY HAPPIEST DAY
MY BRAVEST MOMENT
MY MOST EMBARRASSING MOMENT
THE MYSTERIOUS DAY
THE WORST DAY OF MY LIFE
WHEN I WAS MOST SURPRISED
                  SCARED
                  HAPPY
                  SAD
                  AFRAID
                  PROUD
                  CONFUSED
                  etc.
BEST DAY IN MY FUTURE (make it up)

3. Read your choice of the Children's Sample Poems (included at end) to inspire ideas.

If you are doing this exercise with the entire class, then you'll want to make two or three copies of each "Important Moment" so there will be plenty to go around. It's also a good idea to coordinate the colors with the feelings; for example, putting the more excited feelings on hot or bright colors like yellow and red, and the sad or somber feelings on calm, quiet colors like blue and purple.

4. Invite each child to draw a "moment" from the box and write a poem about it. The "moment" can be used as a title or opening line.

5. If you think a model is needed, here are a few opening lines:

A. I never understood why . . .

B. Everything was fine until . . .

C. My _____ moment happened _____ when I was _____
      place   age

D. I always wanted a day like this . . .

A BAD DAY

A bad day is like when grown-ups are old and have
dents in their faces.
Bad is like when someone steals something of yours
and like when people are mad at their friends.
It's like when men are mad. They look like yellow pizza.
When some people have a bad day they look like a monster
They are mad like a burning stove.

— Rinah Davis, Grade 1

A BAD DAY

As bad as an ant hole.
I felt like yelling.
— Nicole Orio, Grade 1

MY WORST FEAR

I am scared of the devil.
He makes me think about him.
I am scared of the dark.
It looks like fear.
It sounds like an Indian.
He is jumping from the floor and
turns into Dracula in the night.
And he takes us back to the castle
and eats us.

— Tranise Brown, Grade 1

MY BEST DAY

My best day is today.
Today I'm snowing.
My color is white
I taste like ice.
It sounds quiet like when
a dog sleeps.
— Adam Wightman, Grade 2

A NICE NIGHT

The day is full of shining stars
and the night is full of light.
And at night the moon is shining
like lightening bugs.
— Wendy Morales, Grade 2

Images

CAMERA EYES:

This activity is an interesting way to reinforce imagery (making pictures with words), and helps children move effortlessly from simile (a comparison using "like" or "as'") to metaphor (an implied comparison that is more insistent—without "like" or "as"). I usually begin this exercise by asking the class to imagine they have a camera in their foreheads, and every time they blink, they take a picture of what they see. Next I show them an interesting object—preferably one the children haven't seen before; one whose attributes will catch them by surprise—such as a geode, or a beautiful piece of jewelry, or a Slinky that I've set in motion.

1. Invite your children to close their eyes.

2. Hold up the object.

3. Ask them to open their eyes and look steadily at the object for fifteen seconds and take a picture of it in their minds.

4. Put the object out of sight.

5. Write a collaborative (class)

poem where students collectively contribute images (pictures) of what they just saw—*without naming the object.*

> **When you read your collective list of images leave out any "like whats"-then read the entire image list out loud together. Your class poem will have slipped from simile into metaphor quite naturally, and will be a lovely "image" poem.**

Encourage your students to remember colors and textures and the worlds it carries them into. For example, a geode filled with purple and white crystals might appear to be an alien landscape of purple stars, or simply a swirling crystal sea.

A variation of "Camera Eyes" is to take the class on a short walk: around the building, to the library and back, to the flag pole, etc. and ask each child to take at least *three* pictures of objects with their camera eyes. When you return from the walk, put a title on the board:

A. Down _____'s Hallway
      name of school
B. Walk to the Flagpole
C. Around the Playground, etc.

Then ask each class member to contribute *one* picture.

If time permits, you might hand out small strips of paper to the students and ask them to write their images on these. Collect them and make one or two poems by randomly drawing image strips and writing each image on the board.

CAMERA EARS:

This is the "sound" variation of "Camera Eyes" where you plan a sound experience for your class. It can be as simple as thirty seconds of bagpipe music or sound effects, or you might create a live sound experience yourself with bells or a special drum or by tapping on various classroom objects with a pen.

Follow the same process as with "Camera Eyes" and make word pictures for sounds. A favorite sound of mine is no sound—"silence I ask the children to close their eyes and listen to the silence for thirty seconds. I prompt them to *show* silence in their pictures, for example: a polar bear sleeping, a single snowflake floating to the earth, a clock chiming at midnight in an empty house, or a blue candle flickering in a dark room, etc.

Prompt your students to think of quiet things in nature or in weather, or ask them to imagine a single sound in an otherwise still environment.

A variation is to put several "sound" topics on the board, such as "Quiet," "Loud," "Night Sounds," "Morning Sounds," etc. and ask students to write their own "sound" poems.

SCAVENGER SIGHTS AND SOUNDS

With "Scavenger Sights and Sounds" you simply take an unexpected happening and turn it to your class's advantage. For example, a fire drill can provide many sights and sounds worth recording: the sound of the bell, footsteps in the hallway, children flapping their arms on winter days as they wait for the all-clear bell, the silence of waiting, the sound of the flag hardware slapping against the metal flagpole, etc. If you brainstorm these unexpected happenings with your children, you'll get many more ideas than you could imagine yourself. No matter how young they are, I almost always am delighted and surprised by the wealth of ideas the children themselves provide. It makes my job much easier!

Some other happenings you might consider for classroom writing are: sudden storms, an unexpected classroom accident where books or objects clatter to the floor, an animal in the building, a surprise visitor, a loss of power where the lights go off, etc.

CHILDREN'S SAMPLE POEMS:

A NIGHT IN SPRING
The flowers grow slowly
in the moonlight.
The echo of owl runs
through the woods.
The bushes rustle in
the soft wind. And
the trees spread shadows
all over.
— Thomas McCaffery, Grade 3

THE SILENT NIGHT
The night is still,
I can hear myself thinking,
One million things I am
thinking about;
all concentrate on my family
at home,
for I am a white winged angel
— Stefanie Pearl, Grade 4

OUR QUIET POEM

Falling asleep
  in a dark cabin;
When I breathe
  I hear the sea.
A bear snores
  in a deep cave
    and me,
     lost in a
     dream.

Mrs. Byrne's Fourth Grade Collaborative Poem
Gardnertown Elementary

In the dark
I hear the sea
Rushing through a sunken ship.
When I turn a flashlight on
I see stars.
And when I open my eyes for sunrise,
I see moving clouds all over my wall.
When my basketball falls off my shelf,
it turns into a big round cloud.
When day comes
The sun bounces off my shadows,
And turns into all 9 planets
With a big rocket ship flying about.

— Alexis Domenicucci, Grade 4

AS I WAIT

I wait for the
beautiful sunset to arrive
as I wait the day
gets gray and the sun
gets nice and calm.
I wait for that sunset to
melt over the mountain
like butter over a hot
potato.
  I wait

— Melissa Shields, Grade 4

Newspaper Poems

HEADLINERS:

1. GOBBLING GANGSTERS GET TROOPER'S GOAT

2. TOUGH TALK AND TOUGH SENTENCES

3. TWELVE U.S. SENATORS ARE ALIENS

4. BOY FALLS THREE STORIES

5. CLEANER ON WHEELS

6. SWALLOWS RETURN!

7. BURMESE ELEPHANTS PULL BUDDHIST'S TOOTH

8. MIDAIR COLLISION KILLS STAR

9. HUMAN BABIES HATCHED FROM OSTRICH EGGS

10. AT LAST!

These are sample headlines gathered hastily and randomly from newspapers. Any one of these headlines, when taken out of context, provides an intriguing opening line for a poem.

For this activity, the search is half the fun, so bring in a stack of newspapers (any newspapers!) and hand them out to your class. I suggest you divide your students into groups and assign a minimum number of headlines for them to find. Explain that the purpose of the "search" is to provide interesting opening lines for poems, so the more mysterious or intriguing the headline, the better (humor notwithstanding!).

After the search, ask each group them on the board. Choose one and brainstorm with the class. For example, "Swallows Return!" is a perfect opening for a poem about spring. Remind students to listen to their headline's rhythmic patterns. Here's the beginning of a poem I brainstormed recently with a fifth grade:

> Swallows return.
> Daffodils bloom.
> Baseballs fly like
> tiny white moons.
> It's April
> in Pawling
> Spring started today! etc.

If time permits, you might wish to write one "Headliner" poem together as a class before students begin their own poems. Remind students to use their imaginations freely, and not to worry about their chosen headline's relationship to the original newspaper story.

> **The idea of using newspaper headlines as inspiration for poems isn't new. I've used it for years in my classrooms as have a number of my colleagues. If you want a literary treat for yourselves–get a copy of Nancy Willard's poetry collection for adults, WATER WALKER, and see what lyrical wonders she has created from this very exercise.**

to select its three best headlines (or whatever number you wish), and put

CHILDREN'S SAMPLE POEMS:

IN THE GRAVY TRAIN
Deer in the gravy train
Cow in the grayhound bus
Pig in the Delta plane
Chicken in the potato cart
all going to Texas.
— *Allison Woodin, Grade 5*

SIXTH SHOOTER
sixth shooter
five shooter
four shooter
three shooter
two shooter
one shooter
    bang!
— *Brinton Moore, Grade 5*

DRACULA'S SKULL FOUND!

Elvis is lying face down on the ground
Marilyn Monroe is seen in the mall
Tonya Harding is flat on the wall
Nancy Kerrigan's frozen in ice
Janet Jackson has mice
Someone found Frankenstein's brain
Jim Morrison was spotted in Maine
Queen Elizabeth has a gold ring
Bill Clinton was seen in Burger King.
— Anja Brand, Grade 5

CHEFS PUT ON THEIR MITTS

and waitresses got their bats
The Manager put on his umpire mask
And no one makes a sound except the cat.
— A.J. Koola, Grade 5

DISHES RATTLE

Dishes Rattle
Spoons fly
forks spin
and flies die
butterflies dance around in the sky
& birds sing as they soar on by.
me and you walk around town as
bees and bugs buzz around
Then the dishes stop rattling
and the spoons don't fly the
forks stop spinning and the
flies don't die
And as all the things stop
making noise the world stops
turning and no one ever knows.
— Nicole De Pompeis, Grade 5

WINE TALK

Wine Talk
Milk stare
steak chatter
soup chomp
potato gurgle
broccoli burp
coffee sigh
people stunned
all stop
too fast and
get eaten on
the spot.—
— Allison Woodin, Grade 5

POOR GRADES

Good Grades
Dirty Grades
Clean Grades
My Grades
Your Grades
Smart Grades
Unsmart Grades
Some Grades
No Grades
Bad Grades
A lot of Grades
Whew! I'm Tired of Grades!
— Jeff Renwick, Grade 5

THE GHOST OF THE FIREMAN!

The Ghost of the Cat!
The Ghost of the Dog!
The Ghost of the Fish!
The Ghost of the Bird!
The Ghost of the Snake!
The Ghost of the Cow!
The Ghost of the Horse!
The Ghost of the Frog!
The Ghost of Me
Scary young me!
— Chrissy McCormack, Grade 5

ALL MUST GO BY MAY 31ST

The people must
go on dates by
May 31st. Small
dates, big dates.
Movie dates, golf
dates. Dinner dates.
— Laura DeFabbia, Grade 5

JACKIE O DEAD

Jackie O dead
People O know
OOOO no
Jackie O dead
yes it's true
Jackie O dead
OOOOOO   why
Jackie O dead.
— Amy Forzano, Grade 5

WONDERFUL WILD FLOWERS

There are some wonderful
wild flowers. They are wild
as wild cats. The flowers
are orange and white.
They are orange as the
first orange. The wind
pushes it back and forth
slowly.
— Laura DeFabbia, Grade 5

Dictionary Games

DICTIONARY NAMES:

This exercise unites a dictionary search with a whimsical exploration of character. Even though this activity works well for both single or multi-groupings, I suggest you allow students to work in pairs, because an exchange of ideas will lend momentum to their search for words as well as a more thorough brainstorming of characteristics for their "word" people.

1. Have your students look up several two-or three-syllable words in the dictionary that could be turned into names.

2. Ask them to write the words down with a brief definition for each.

3. Next ask them to divide the words into syllables to form a first name and a last name, for example: Miss Polly Wog for polliwog; Mr. Bill Board for billboard, etc.

4. Put the following model on the board to show how a poem/ story can evolve from each name:

Mr./Miss/Ms. _____
name

is a man/woman of _____ years

with _____ like (option)
      describe the person

She wears _____

and likes to _____
      favorite activity/job

Miss/Mr. _____ lives _____
                 place/city

with _____
      whom or what

and is _____
      person's feeling about self/life

with/about _____ etc.

> **When possible, ask your students to incorporate the dictionary word's meaning into the person's characteristics (as with Willy Nilly). Also, keep an atlas handy so students can search for surprising names of cities and towns for their characters (as in Rabbit Hatch, Kentucky-a real town!).**

Encourage your children to add whatever details they like to their poems: favorite foods, friends, how people respond (do they like or dislike the character), pet peeves, interesting habits, etc.

Here are two sample poems to read to the class:

Miss Polly Ester (polyester)
is a woman of 60
with puffy white hair that
billows like a cloud around
her face.
She wears big black shoes

and flowered dresses and
bowls every Wednesday
with her ladies' club.
Miss Ester lives in a
small yellow house with
her son, Al, and two
chihuahuas.
She is happy with
her life.

Mr. Willy Nilly (willynilly)
is a man of 22
    with short blonde hair and
    gold rimmed glasses.
He wears brown suits with
no ties, and his socks
never match.
He's always in a hurry.
You can see him every morning
racing to work with his coat
half on and papers falling
from his briefcase.
He loves to travel, but
frequently misses the plane.
He lives in Rabbit Hatch,
Kentucky,
and invents kitchen gadgets
in his spare time.
    He's usually not sure if he's
coming or going.

Dictionary Name Samples:

kowtow	rollicking
marigold	lily-livered
periwinkle	rondeau
scrimshaw	limburger
relax	solfeggio
shish-kebab	lima bean
alloy	almanac
coriander	tomato
bigwig	billboard
coracoid	linseed
philharmonic	angel
croquette	polliwog
crisscross	daffodil
vivacious	willy-nilly
jack o' lantern	

I often find it helpful for younger students to have some pre-fixes that easily lend themselves to forming names. You might suggest or assign a few of the following pre-fixes to facilitate your class's dictionary search.

ben-	cora-	jon-
con-	peg-	cor-
sol-	jes-	rod-
phil-	carl-	ann-
lil-	ros-	sil-
pete-	de-	stan-
viv-	syl-	al-
car-	wil-	nar-
id-	sam-	rock-
wes-	star-	tim-
tom-	les-	lin-
poly-	pol-	mar-
vi-	ed-	len-
lily-	petti-	

I HOLD IN MY HANDS:

This is an exercise in adjectives—lots of them! Read the following poem to your students (take a deep breath first), then break out the dictionaries.

Next put a model on the board:

I hold in my hands
one _____

_____

_____
piece of myself.
If you look closely
you can see it.

Ask students to fill the middle of the poem with adjectives chosen gleefully and carefully from the dictionary. Next ask them to make the structure "skinny"—letting each

---

LOOK CLOSELY

I hold in my hands
one invaluable, unusually large, circular,
hydrated, cellular, fish-spined, shell-pasted,
molecular, wood-fitted, lilac-scented, pollinated,
earth-colored, Katanga-mined, Bantu-smelted,
cleaned, polished, rough-edged, curved,
granite, gold-encrusted, filigreed, stamped,
platinum inlaid, green-embossed, diamond-tipped,
rectangular, sculpted, Polynesian-carved,
interconnecting, figure-locking,
beaten, Persian-hammered, sheeted,
fur-covered, feathered,
braided, Inca-woven, lace-trimmed,
stitched, beaded, Navajo embroidered,
Chinese-inspired, Japanese-designed, Brahmanic,
blue-lacquered, hand-painted, red-enameled,
impenetrable, soaring, mythic, hermaphroditic,
Hebraic, gothic,
mobile, eurythmic, mechanical,
non-plastic, free-spinning,
winged, elevated,
piece of myself.

If you look closely
you can see it.

— Morton Marcus

---

adjective find its own spot on the page. (You might wish to set a specific number of adjectives.) Then share each poem with gusto.

For adventurous souls I always encourage variations. You can do this by altering the poem model slightly. For example:

I hold in my _____
       head
       heart
       mind
       hand
       dreams, etc.

one _____ of my _____
if you _____
you can _____

CHILDREN'S SAMPLE POEMS:

I HOLD IN MY BACKYARD

I hold in my backyard
some bramble bangled Christmas lights,
Fable faced hectigonic facets of fairy
shrimps and flabbergasted fadish
radishes, whirly and ingenious gems of
gawky, gavotting wind chime, A
gift of giggling german germs of
green lettering terrified, A lake
of gill rakes, fat cats in a lawn
chair, giant gibberish, a frosted
gypsy with a gibulative girl
with a swirling bomper baubled
girdle. No way I can't find
an atrocious, white, little bit
of oregano!
And it's all in my backyard!
             — Jessica Gallo, Grade 5

DREAMS

I hold in my hands   one
vain, savvy, phlegmatic, vain-
glorious, golden, engraved,
delicately shaped,
in a grotto with a frond,
enchanted, jeweled
       piece of myself.
If you look closely at my dreams
you will see another world.
         — Adam Bloom, Grade 5

IN MY HAND

In my hand I hold one glass-
textured, African painted, glossy covered, gold
plated, crystal tipped, circular, perfectionated,
blossom scented, feathery, zestful, zigodic, zetaed,
bondering, single glass bead. If you peer
closely, you will see it.
           — Jillian Utter, Grade 5

THE BRAIN

I hold in my skull one supercolossal
unwashed, extra intelligent, reliable,
unstoppable, gold plated, argon-
filled, gas-powered, football-
shaped, orange-colored, 212°,
unchanged, logical,
perfect, licensed,
electronically,
fuel-injected,
piece of
my brain.
Don't
try
to
out-
think
me!

— Lou Ernst, Grade 5

ON MY FACE

are two
     blood shot
     blue-pupiled
     white-irised
     bright
     reflective
     moving
     curious
     excited
     round
     amazing
     exploring
     absorbing
     wet
     sometimes teary
     sometimes closed
     sensitive
        EYES!
        If you look closely you can see
my blood-shot, blue pupiled, white irised,
bright, reflective, moving, curious, excited,
round, amazing, exploring, absorbing, wet,
sometimes teary, sometimes closed, sensitive eyes
                  — Paul Plekon

Edibles

If Food Were Clothing:

As teachers well know, children are gastronomically oriented little beings, and the younger the child, the more dominant food's influence as a force in his or her life. Filling a stomach with something—sometimes anything!—is never far from a second or third grader's mind; hence, the necessary inclusion of a chapter about food.

"If Food Were Clothing" is very popular with younger children, but be prepared for lots of giggling, because for some reason, the idea of wearing food or eating their clothing tickles their funny bones. Therefore,

I usually begin this activity with a solemn tone, because it's even funnier when the children figure out what this exercise is really about.

1. Ask a student to stand in front of the class. Explain that you are conducting an experiment with colors.

2. Point to an article of the child's clothing and create a food simile for it. For example: "Tom's hat is blue like blueberry pie. His shirt is green like a plateful of spinach."

3. Repeat this procedure with other articles of Tom's clothing—subtly leaving out the "like" of the simile format and changing each comparison to a metaphor.

4. Next read the following poem to the students to give them ideas before they write their own edible clothing poems.

EDIBLE

My shirt is red tomato soup.
My pockets are green peas.
My khakis are brown dog biscuits.
My socks are cottage cheese.
I have vanilla ice-cream shoes
with limp spaghetti bows.
I wish I could eat everything,
but then I'd have no clothes!
                    — Jacqueline Sweeney

If you think your students need more prompting, put a simple model on the board that mimics the above poem.

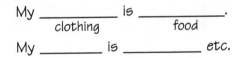

FOOD MUSIC:

You might begin this exercise by playing a clarinet solo and then asking what food it makes your students think of; or you might pass out food samples (apple slices, potato chips, squares of chocolate) one at a time and ask the children to close their eyes as they are tasting and see what music it inspires in their minds. As they chew, break down the food's qualities for them, for example, an apple: its smooth skin, its sweetness, its crunch, etc.

> **If you're outside on a field trip, whether in the countryside or city, you might follow this same process with nature or architecture. And while traveling on a bus, never underestimate the culinary impact of passing scenery, road signs, and cars.**

I recently did this activity with a fifth grade class whose chorus and concert band were performing that evening, so the music was overflowing in their minds and feelings. With this class I skipped handing out food samples and immediately began brainstorming musical instruments and musical groups. After a mighty list that included everything from cowbells to a grand piano, I put the following models on the board:

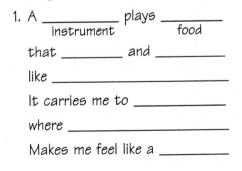

2. _____ is/are_____
("Like What") food   music
   It _____like _____

Next I read the following "Food Music" poem to inspire thinking:

FOOD MUSIC

A clarinet plays gravy
that's brown and bubbly
like the deep Mississippi
and carries me to
a forest of winding
snakes and long
looping vines.
It makes me feel
like a dark leaf
        on a
                quiet tree.

The crunch of an apple
is tiny bells;
its sweetness
is violins.
Notes glissando
as down it goes—
smooth skin sliding
like trombones
        through my stomach
                my veins
                        my life.
                —Jacqueline Sweeney

CHILDREN'S SAMPLE POEMS:

CLARINET

A clarinet plays whipped
cream that swirls down through
the inside and comes to your ears
to taste the delicious music. It
carries me to a concert hall where
I play in front of millions of people.
The people will eat the whipped cream
through their ears.
                —Lauren Palladino, Grade 5

MILK CHOCOLATE

Milk chocolate
is like an oboe
on a cold dark
night. It takes
me inside the earth's
spirit where all the
earth's love is.
                —Kyle Lyon, Grade 5

OLÉ

A cowbell is like steak
getting back from the
butcher's and sounds like
"Hernando's Hideaway"
                Olé
                —Kyle Lyon, Grade 5

WHAT MY PIANO PLAYS

My piano plays strawberries like small red fish spitting water at you. It sound like smooth, classic music that guides me to another land where instruments can play anything.

— Michelle Leo, Grade 5

TRUMPET FOOD

A trumpet plays spaghetti that is as twirly as the hottest water. My instrument sounds like an ending of a song. My trumpet plays spaghetti as steaming as a bucket of hot water.
It leads me to the Amazon River
where I meet Native Americans washing their clothes.
It makes me feel like one of the tribe.
I start to be like them. Then we get to know each other.

— Jonathan Price, Grade 5

Sour apples are like grunge music. It tastes normal but once you start to chew you feel the sour blend on your tongue. Then you squint your face in a displace and for a few seconds it's the best thing in the world.

— Vincent Galvin, Grade 5

HOW TO EAT A POEM:

This activity acquires its name from the poem by Eve Merriam and is a great exercise to do with a class at the end of a poetry unit, because it gives children the opportunity to think about what poems are really made of in both concrete and abstract terms, and what poems mean to them. It also allows students to transform poetry's language of feeling and experience into a gastronomical happening.

1. Read the following poem to your class to set the tone, and, forgive me, the *flavor* of this activity:

HOW TO EAT A POEM

Don't be polite.
Bite in.
Pick it up with your fingers and lick the juice
    that may run down your chin.
It is ready and ripe now, whenever you are.
You do not need a knife or fork or spoon
or plate or napkin or tablecloth
For there is no core
or stem
or rind
or pit
or seed
or skin
to throw away.

— Eve Merriam

---

2. Next, with or without the aid of a thesaurus, assist your students "to brainstorm" a list of strong and interesting verbs

for the action EAT. Call this LIST ONE and put it on the left side of the board, leaving room for another list beside it.

Words I've used in LIST ONE:

munch	dribble	gargle
stir	crunch	drool
gurgle	spoon	nibble
chomp	swallow	fork
gobble	devour	empty
cut	inhale	chew
fill	swirl	gnaw
digest	mix	twirl
slurp	spit out	mash
strain		

3. Brainstorm a list of poetry-related words with your class, being sure to offer plenty of your own sample words—especially abstract ones—because this realm is often difficult for children to enter at first without a little prompting. Label this LIST TWO and put on the board beside LIST ONE.

Words I've used in LIST TWO:

words	happiness	magic
secrets	nouns	sadness
mystery	inside	adjectives
colors	imagination	outside
verbs	senses	dreams
vowels	action	feelings
pleasure	consonants	rhyme
simile	safely	syllables
meter	alliteration	hope
sounds	rhythm	tastes
smells	metaphors	

Be sure to include in your list any poetry terms you've discussed in class, as well as any ideas, feelings, objects written about in poems, etc. the children would like to include.

4. When it's time to write, show your students how to create opening lines for their poems by placing a word from each list side by side, and then adding the word "like," which will form a simile when the line is completed.

For example:

_____ _____ like _____
List One List Two

Samples:

Slurp similes like _____

Gobble verbs like _____

Nibble hope and joy like _____

With older children (grades four and five), you might wish to add LIST THREE to their thinking—a list of ADJECTIVES relating to both poetry and food. Ask students to "sprinkle" some of these into their poems to enhance their descriptions.

Words I used in LIST THREE:

mysterious	gooey	tough
chocolate	strange	sloppy
soft	strawberry	dark
drippy	sweet	fried
light	crispy	juicy
flavorful	magical	crunchy
salty	nutritious	imaginative
tasty	delicious	bountiful
hot	scrumptious	nourishing
salivating	cold	aromatic
dripping	steaming	

Before they write, remind your children that they are giving directions about how to eat a poem, so it's okay to sound forceful. I'd also suggest you read the following samples by other children to help stimulate ideas.

CHILDREN'S SAMPLE POEMS:

HOW TO EAT A POEM
Munch on a Metaphor!
Scarf the sounds!
Fork some feelings!
Gnaw the nouns!
Mash mystery and magic!
Let dreams' juice dribble down your chin!
Blaa! Hurl the hope!
Then eat it all again!
— Halsey McGowan, Grade 5

HOW TO EAT A POEM

Attack its greatness like you haven't
eaten for days. Gobble its mystifying
magic like you've been on a diet
and you've gotten your first taste
of junk food for weeks. Take its
loveliness and slowly make it
last like you would a chocolate
cake, eat it any way you want
for the way you do it will always
be right.

— Travis Gale, Grade 3

HOW TO
EAT A POEM

Gnaw on colors as if they
were sweet cherries dripping with
its luscious red dye. Slurp its
Dreams of candies and sweets as
if they were your own. Devour
its darkness as if it were dark
Chocolate pudding dripping off your
spoon. Gnaw the imagination into
fantasies. And when you're done,
eat more.

— Brandon Nikola, Grade 5

HOW TO EAT A POEM

Stuff similes
    like you'll never
        get anything that tastes
           like it again. Blobber at
               the words like mad. Bargle it
                  around like syllables. Let
metaphors
           Seep into your mouth. Surge
        into your stomach. If
    you don't like
the power
      spit it out
        just like beets. Inhale
           its magic aroma. Crunch the
             colors and swallow bite by bite.
               — Jennifer Cichocki, Grade 3

HOW TO EAT A POEM

Pig out. Don't worry about how disgraceful
    You look!
Throw similes in your mouth and
    Squish them through your teeth!
Spit chewed metaphors across the room.
    chew like a cow.
After your meal eat junk food,
    Inhale candybars, popcorn, and puddings,
Cakes, Jellos, and ice cream!
    Then after you're so full you
    Can't talk anymore, throw-up
And start all over again.
       — Amy Quesnel, Grade 3

HOW TO EAT A POEM

Nibble on the fantasies like a piece of fat on
a liver dinner that you don't like.
Feast on the feelings that scare you in your
dreams. Munch on the sounds
like a wet steak with ketchup. Shred the
darkness into hope, like a secret no one
told·you. Rip apart the mystery like butter on
a mashed potato. And don't
stop until you're done.
       — Randi Licari, Grade 5

I'M SO MAD I COULD SCREAM!:

One of my favorite ways to defuse an angry child or situation is to read William Cole's poem "I'm So Mad I Could Scream" to a class. I've discovered that teachers also like this poem because it's not only cathartic, but it shows children they're not alone with their angry feelings; that everyone at one time or another wants to beat up mother and dad—and little brother and big sister, too! When I read this poem I *always* address this by saying: "I'm forty-three years old, and sometimes I still feel this way towards my mom and dad. But that's what I like about poetry. I can write about my thoughts and get those feelings out without hurting anyone—or getting into trouble."

The ending of William Cole's poem is worth worlds, because it offers a nonviolent way to resolve anger, and ends with the feeling of relief; the kind that usually follows a safe, healthy expression of negative feelings.

I'M SO MAD I COULD SCREAM!
I'm so mad I could scream,
I'm so mad I could spit,
Turn over a table,
Run off in a snit!

I'm so mad I could yell,
I could tear out my hair,
Throw a rock through a window,
Or wrestle a bear!

I mean— I am furious,
In a terrible huff,
I'm raging and roaring
And boy, am I tough!

I'm really ferocious,
I really am *mad*.
I'm ready to beat up
My mother and dad!

On thinking it over,
I *will* not leave home,
But I'll put all my anger
Right here in this poem.

I'm feeling much better—
Like peaches and cream—
For a poem is the best way
Of letting off steam!
                    — William Cole

I usually follow this with a poem written by my son, Matt, when he was six years old and suffering daily in kindergarten at the hands of an aggressive fellow student. I explain to the children how Matt felt much better after being "allowed" to write about all the destructive things he'd like to do—in poem form—and how it was actually better, because he didn't get in trouble (when I say this last part, half of the class is usually nodding in solemn agreement!).

MAD
I'm so mad I could
spit spikes into a wall
and crush the ceiling
down which would
make the walls fall.
I could beat the chalkboard in
and tear books into little pieces
and feed them to the sharks.
Mad tastes like
rotten orange juice
and makes me feel
like stale dried up
gum mixed with
food coloring and dirt.
                    — Matt Piperno, Age 6

Here are two simple models:

1. I'm So _____
   I could _____
   I'm so _____
   I could _____ etc.

2. When I'm _____
   I feel like a _____

I find it helpful to remind the children as they are writing to remember the "Like What" List to help them create pictures or images for their feelings. Also, it's sometimes quite helpful for younger children to brainstorm a list of feelings they'd like you to put on the board. Be sure to add some of your own if the list seems paltry, for example—"Left Out" or "Frustrated" or "Sleepy"—because students don't always think of these.

Next read some sample poems by other children. This is especially important to set up this exercise, because your class will relax when they hear you read about some of the more "controversial" feelings as the center of poems. It's as if you are saying to them: "Yes, it's okay to feel what you are feeling. And it's also okay to write about it."

CHILDREN'S SAMPLE POEMS:

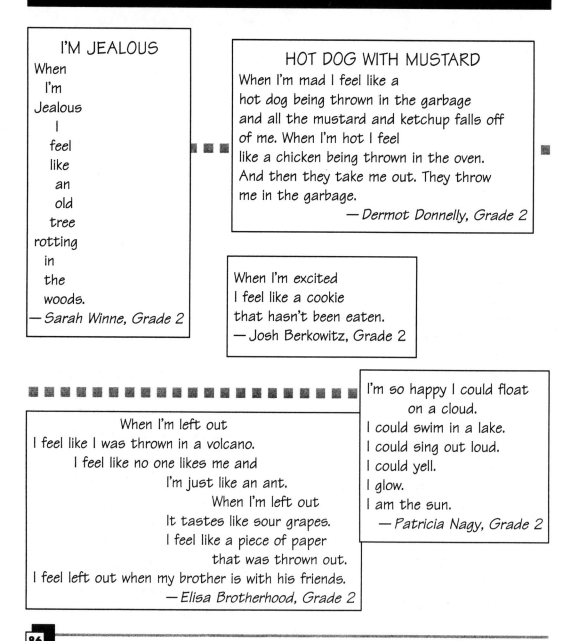

I'M JEALOUS
When
  I'm
Jealous
   I
    feel
    like
     an
    old
    tree
rotting
  in
  the
  woods.
— Sarah Winne, Grade 2

HOT DOG WITH MUSTARD
When I'm mad I feel like a
hot dog being thrown in the garbage
and all the mustard and ketchup falls off
of me. When I'm hot I feel
like a chicken being thrown in the oven.
And then they take me out. They throw
me in the garbage.
— Dermot Donnelly, Grade 2

When I'm excited
I feel like a cookie
that hasn't been eaten.
— Josh Berkowitz, Grade 2

When I'm left out
I feel like I was thrown in a volcano.
I feel like no one likes me and
I'm just like an ant.
When I'm left out
It tastes like sour grapes.
I feel like a piece of paper
that was thrown out.
I feel left out when my brother is with his friends.
— Elisa Brotherhood, Grade 2

I'm so happy I could float
on a cloud.
I could swim in a lake.
I could sing out loud.
I could yell.
I glow.
I am the sun.
— Patricia Nagy, Grade 2

MISERABLE

Miserable is when I fall into
a
big
mud
puddle
And my sister gets a piece of
candy and I get none.
Miserable is
when
my
dime
goes
into
a big black hole and now I
feel like a red flower getting
stepped on.
— Jennifer Banach, Grade 3

I am so Excellent I could
climb a mountain.
I fall on a cliff.
Sometimes I just lay there
like a bad man.
I am so Excellent I could
kill all my feelings
inside me.
And sometimes they kill me.
— Edward Bowling, Grade 3

WHEN I FEEL MAD

Mad is red like red hot peppers
And is also like blood bursting out of my ears.
When I am mad I feel like I could throw a baseball at a car.
When I am mad I like to close my door and put on some clown music
and it usually calms me down.
— Timothy McCormick, Grade 3

PLACES TO HIDE:

If something embarrassing happens to someone in your class there are two things you might do.

1. Ask the entire class to write one poem each about the most embarrassing thing that ever happened to them, being sure to include how other people reacted and how it made them feel.;

• Did the people laugh?
• Did they say mean things?
• What did they say?

2. Ask the embarrassed child to describe how he/she feels right now:

- "I feel like a crayon getting colored with."
- "I feel like a dog having no fun, and nobody wants to pet me."
- "I feel like a flower getting picked."

Then ask the child to tell where he/she would like to hide: (Name at least two places)

I'd like to hide in the _____
where it is _____ as _____
<u>dark, cold</u>

I'd like to hide _____
where it is _____
like _____

I'd like to hide far away from _____

Then I'd feel better.

3. Share everyone's embarrassing moment writings—ending with a sharing of the embarrassed child's feelings and places to hide. (You might wish to read the last poem).

LETTER TO MYSELF

Have you ever had a child so angry or sad or disappointed that no matter what you say, nothing will console him—much less get him back on track with the rest of the class? And what about those personal disputes between two students that go on for days and seem to develop lives of their own? And what about those unexpected tragedies that affect an entire class—such as when a teacher or classmate dies? These situations might utilize this activity, "Letter to Myself," which simply allows a child to say to himself or herself what he really needs to hear. The sharing of this letter isn't always as important as the process of writing it, but when possible, it's helpful for both the student and/or the rest of the class if the letter(s) is (are) shared.

1. Give the student two pieces of paper—just in case—because this process shouldn't be interrupted, once it's begun, not even to ask for more paper!

2. Ask the child to date the paper—as with a letter—and then write:

Dear _____
<u>student's own name</u>

3. Next ask the student to say all the things he wishes someone would say to him.

NOTE: The only requirement is the letter must include *three* wishes related to the current situation.

Model:

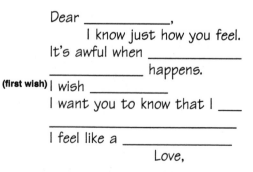

Dear _____,
     I know just how you feel.
It's awful when _____
_____ happens.
(first wish) I wish _____
I want you to know that I ___
_____
I feel like a _____
           Love,

Believe it or not, some teachers have found this technique so helpful that they've designed their own "letters to myself" format and keep copies on hand for any sad, angry, or surprising situations that may occur in their classrooms. For example, what would you do if your discovered on a Monday morning that your class's cherished gerbil had died? These letters provide a vehicle for the collective sharing of grief.

One teacher I know encouraged her students to use at least two "like whats" in their letters of disappointment over the sudden cancellation of a long-awaited class trip due to inclement weather. I must admit, never before have I heard snow described with such vehement similes.

SITUATIONAL "WHAT IFS":

The "What If" format isn't new (I offer some "what if" configurations in *Teaching Poetry, Yes You Can!*). Ogden Nash, John Ciardi, and Shel Silverstein, to name a few, have written "What If" poems. I've simply directed my "What If" lessons as specific vehicles for learning.

"Situational What Ifs" are versatile, require no brainstorming, and are the perfect "plug-ins" for a lengthy bus ride, or any in-school or out-of-school situation where you and your children must unexpectedly wait for unknown minutes (hours!)—due to anything from delayed photo snaps on picture-taking day to school evac-

uated emergencies. And don't forget that stalled elevator!

The premise is simple: Use whatever "delay" situation in which you find yourself and your class as subject matter—then propose two or three "what ifs" to your class in rapid succession. For example:

* What if this bus never stopped?
* What if it bumped all the way to _____?
* What if it sprouted metal wings and flew?
* What if all the people in this museum line turned into trees? (flowers, animals, plants, etc.)
* What kind of tree would you be?
* I'd be a Maple because of my red coat and swaying arms.

Once you've engaged your class's attention the "what if" process teaches itself. While sharing the children's "what ifs," stop after the intriguing questions and have your class try to answer them. After all, what *would* happen if the bus never stopped?

It's Spring!

This is one of those writing exercises where I blitz the children with lots of poems about spring and *any* related themes: trees, plants, weeds, flowers, the environment, ecology, etc. Everyone studies ecology and the environment in spring because of Earth Day, so themes of ecological awareness creep into the children's poetry, and I get poems about everything from being inside a rose to endangered species.

Every year I find new poems to read for this exercise by going through anthologies, and I try to include thematic poems that contain strong verbs, similes and refrain—and then step

back curiously when each class writes to see what ideas the children choose to use in their own poems.

You might wish to put a few opening lines on the board for reference, but don't limit the children to these—let them jump into their poems any way that suits them.

Some opening lines I've used:

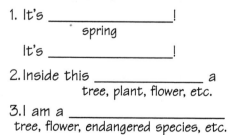

1. It's _____!
           spring

   It's _____!

2. Inside this _____ a
          tree, plant, flower, etc.

3. I am a _____
   tree, flower, endangered species, etc.

I've included a variety of children's sample poems here, so there are plenty of options to choose from should you wish to concentrate on a single theme like plants or endangered species, or the earth. There are certainly enough poems here to use as the entire set-up—should you not have the time to look up spring poems of your own.

As the children write their poems, I sometimes put up a checklist to remind them to look through their poems for the following:

- colors
- strong verbs
- an interesting title
- an ending

Some suggested endings:

- perhaps . . .
- makes me feel . . .
- I wish . . .

You'd be surprised how this little checklist encourages students to make their poems stronger.

CHILDREN'S SAMPLE POEMS:

A WHOLE NEW WORLD INSIDE A ROSE

Inside a rose there are two
different worlds.
    I look up and
see happiness inside
the blossom
    I look down
and see anger in
the thorny stem
    a bee comes along
and enters the blossom
to fill up its happiness
the happiness is attached
to its legs like
yellow pollen
    a roach comes
along and touches
the thorny stem
its anger is filled
and it goes out to
    find its supper.
        — David Riley, Grade 5

THE SPRING THAT CAME

It's spring and the flowers are chuckling
just like the morning teapot. The trees
are dancing in the bright yellow sun
like the paint on my wall. The green
grass sings in the wind just like my
voice in the air the water that flows
in my hair It's spring.
        — Steven Strong, Grade 5

INSIDE A FLOWER

Inside a flower is water
that goes into the seed.
Opens up into a bud.
The bud opens up
into a flower, so I
push my way up in
the seed, then I
push my way up in
into the bud and
up I go and there I am.
        — Ashly Herman, Grade 2

SPRING TIME

It's Spring
It's time
to sing the poem of clementine
to cry and whine
for lemonade
and chocolate nuts filled with
marmalade to
run and jump
around the flowers
prancing dancing
with the sun
but then it ends
with
sorrow and pain
for the sun has
tired out
and snow
is starting to fall
oh yes,
it ain't spring no more!

— James Kimma, Grade 5

A GROWING FLOWER'S LIFE

I am a flower seed little
as a cell in the deep hard
ground, the ground is like
brown cake mix not yet
baked, but ready to be. I am
sprouting up and out through the
ground
like a doctor pulling out teeth.
My stem is getting bigger and
fatter as I break up through
the ground. My flower colors are
coming out and my buds are opening
up like opening a paint can.
I smell beautiful like a
petunia. The grass is dancing
at my beautifulness, they are
dancing because of me. The trees
are jumping up and down
at my beautifulness, they are
jumping because of me. The clouds
are smiling at my beautifulness,
they are smiling because of me.
Everyone likes me because I'm
now a full-grown flower.

— Jason Chipkin, Grade 5

THE NAME OF THE ROSE

Inside a rose
I see passion and deceit
I see beautiful velvet petals
below my brown shoes
The beautiful aroma fills my
nose like a shining black king
snake. I go through labyrinths of
blood red walls.
When I go through I think
of
anger and
fierceness.
I feel
I'm lost for eternity.

— Luciano Valdivia, Grade 5

LITTLE FISH

I am a fish swimming calm.
I am golden brown
with a slash of copper.
My eyes are diamonds.
I wish the water was clean.
So I can dance around.

— Victoria Vanzo, Grade 2

GOLDEN SKY

The golden is hidden
  in the waves
of light, as seaweed
    trees
      start
    to
      fight,
  puffy fish come in
and out and wave their
scaly tails about, spaghetti and
  salt
    ring
up the crew and sing a
  song to you,
wind from boats pollute
  the air
    I say,
  "hey there
    don't
pollute the air."
— Anna Ditton, Grade 2

THE GIANT OF THE WORLD

The giant of the
WORLD
I have a whale inside
me. The whale lives in
my mouth. It sings the
whale song. It is a secret
because I am a whale and
I sing the whale's song.
I feel proud that I am
  a giant of the world that
  is free.
— Katie Biamonte, Grade 2

A TREE

I am a tree blowing
in the air
with my branches
singing for sun
singing for food
singing for water.
— Diana D'muro, Grade 2

THE CHANGED EARTH

The earth is a beautiful place where the flowers
and weeds sway like young teenagers dancing
where the rocks stand still like a game of freeze
tag. Where the trees slowly rock back and forth like
an old woman knitting in her rocking chair. Where
the weeds slowly emerge and stretch their
arms like a child stretching in the morning.
Where the water trickles like water dripping
from a faucet. Where the air slowly blows
like a baby crawling across the floor. Where
the soil is as brown as the bark of the
tree and it stays still like an old man reading his
paper. But, then you turn
your back and everything is destroyed by
humans.
— Alissa Stoever, Grade 5

Kingdoms

POWER POEM:

This activity gives children the opportunity to choose and direct their personal power as the self-proclaimed rulers of kingdoms they themselves design. Before starting, tell the children they'll need to make choices, and to think carefully about the following questions:

1. What is the kingdom made of?
- jewels
- spiders
- weather (sunlight, snow, great winds, etc.)
- trees
- colors
- animals (or one specific type of animal)
- food etc.

2. As the ruler of the kingdom, what do you look like?

Eyes	Clothing
stars	silk
ice	clouds
laser rays	gold
rubies	vegetation

(You might brainstorm similar lists for hair, etc.)

3. What is your name?
- Splish-Splosh the Rain Queen
- Oonie Moonie the Planet King

- GilaGuana the Lizard Lord etc.

4. What powers do you have?

- to make all animals do your bidding?
- to turn all matter to sand?
- to control weather?

5. How do you use these powers?

- to destroy things?
- to build things?
- to help your subjects/
- to harm your subjects? etc.

6. Do you have any special rules for your kingdom?

7. Do your subjects:

- love you?
- fear you?
- dislike you?

8. How do you *feel* as this ruler with all this power?

9. Do you have any wishes?

After posing these questions, read the following poem: (note: "Dien Tamaela" is a girl's name)

You'll be surprised at the interesting, occasionally subterranean realms that emerge from this activity.

A TALE FOR DIEN TAMAELA

I am Pattiradjawane* (*pah-tee-rah-djah-WAH-nay)
Whom the gods watch over
I alone.

I am Pattiradjawane
Foam of the sea.
The sea is my blood.

I am Pattiradjawane
When I was born
The gods brought me an oar.

I am Pattiradjawane, guarding the nutmeg groves.
I am fire on the shore. Whoever comes near
Must call my name three times.

In the night-time quiet, seaweed dances
To the sound of my drum,
Nutmeg trees become maidens' bodies
And live till dawn.

Dance!
Be happy!
Forget everything!

But take care not to make me angry
I'll kill the nut trees, stiffen the maidens
I'll bring down the gods!

I'm in the night, in the day,
In the rhythm of the seaweed and in the fire
that roasts the island . . .

I am Pattiradjawane
Whom the gods watch over
I alone.

Chiril Anwar

(translated from the Indonesian by Burton Raffel)

QUACKADAC

My name is Quackadac. I am huge.
I have yellow hair. The color of my scales
is purple and I am mean. I smell like
soap. I have claws. My kingdom is big
and brown. It is under the ground.
When I get mad, my scales
stand. I breathe fire when I get
mad. I guard the red ruby.
Nothing can get past me. I am
the strongest living thing and I
am the ruler of time. I am
hot-blooded. I will kill anything that
comes 5 inches close to me.
— *John Damian, Grade 3*

CASTLE UNIVERSE

I am the king of everything;
My name is Walla-Walla-Wing-Wang.
I can do anything I please.
I am the King of Kings.
I have a luxurious Kingdom.
I call it Castle Universe (It is made of clouds of glory)
I have powers beyond any human ability.
I can do anything and with my
powers I can never be defeated.
My eyes are lightening bolts and
My head is a star.
I have no body or legs because
I float.
I use my powers for self-defense
and any old reason.
NO ONE TALKS WHEN Walla-Walla-Wing-Wang talks!
NO ONE LOOKS AT THE KING!
My subjects are loyal and if they aren't
they will be beheaded.
Yes, I am Walla-Walla-Wing-Wang.
— *A.J. Koola, Grade 5*

SUNGARIA'S KINGDOM

I'm Sungaria the Great
　　With my golden blood
Running through my lead veins
　　My copper-lined bones
Creates my body.
　　At times I am strong
Other times weak
　　At times I stand tall
Other times short
　　My mood changes my
characteristics
　　I rule all of Ziggut
A far kingdom where New York
　　Once stood 3000 years ago
I rule the weather and
　　environment
My kingdom stays the same
　　and for ever more
I'm everlasting
　　For ever I will rule
the people of Ziggut
　　For they love me.
　　My people enjoy their life
They bring me baskets of fine
　　cheeses and wine
But my life is sad
　　I'm never to show myself to anyone.
I wish I could rule my own life
　　But my people rule me
This saddens my life
　　That I rule everyone
Everyone but me!
　　　　　— Marcus Bands,
　　　　　　Grade 5

"CIEN"

My name is "Cien" (100 in Spanish)
I am very powerful, I can rule over man
I rule over the Kingdom Zierra.
Our clothing is made of thin, rich silk
The color of our clothes is blue and white
My eyes are as blue as the morning sky.
My skin is as soft as cotton.
When I cry I cry roses.
When my people are good I
cry because I am happy and
I give them roses. When they
are bad I scream as loud as thunder.
My subjects are very loyal.
I feel they feel as happy as me.
　　　　　— Myra Sanchez, Grade 5

HOOTFACE

My name is Hootface. I am ugly
like worms. When people see me,
they scream. I am red like blood.
When I see people I get mad. I
feel like boiling over.
　　I live on a hill.
　　　　　— Rachael Malach, Grade 3

BENEBOPER

My name is Beneboper and I look like
a butterfly with pink eyes, blue wings,
and orange fuzzy antennae. I am the
ruler of the Benes. When the Benes
disobey me, I bop them on the head.
But when they are good, I invite them
to dinner in my palace. I eat goodies
and sweets, and I have 2,300,105 cavities
I am a good ruler don't you think so?
　　　　　— Matthew Sataloff, Grade 4

Explorations

WHAT WILL YOU FIND?

LANDSCAPE

What will you find at the edge of the world?
A footprint,
a feather,
desert sand swirled?
a rain of stars,
or a junkyard of cars?

What will there be at the rim of the earth?
A mollusk,
a mammal,
a new creature's birth?
Eternal sunrise,
immortal sleep,
or cars piled up in a rusty heap?
— Eve Merriam

This activity is based on the Eve Merriam poem, "Landscape," and is refreshing because of its use of questions to induce thinking.

I like how this poem lends itself to a whole language approach to many subject areas. Notice how Eve Merriam suggests imaginative possibilities for what we might find at the edge of the world. Your students, in turn, might pose questions about what they'll find:

- in the twinkle of a star
- in the scale of a dragon
- in the heart of a giant
- in the center of a cloud
- in the middle of an avalanche
- in a black hole
- in the Sea of Tranquility
- in the stomach of a shark
- in the middle of an igloo
- in the eye of a hurricane
- in the center of the earth
- in the middle of a nightmare
- in the center of love/hate/ fear/war/peace/prejudice, etc.

Children may blend fact with fantasy as they pose their questions about outer space, habitats, ecosystems, historical scenes, etc. You might wish to confine your "What will you find . . ?" explorations to one current subject area and brainstorm that together as a class before writing.

Here is a model:

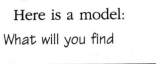

What will you find

_____?

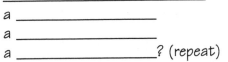

a _____

a _____

a _____? (repeat)

This structure might be too confining for some students to flex their imaginations as they'd like. Encourage these students to create their own structures after choosing one of the topics (or making up their own topics). Endings, for example, need not be humorous, and posed questions can maintain a serious tone throughout the poem. You can reinforce subject-verb agreement with younger students by stressing how the verbs 'is' and 'are' must change in order to agree with either a singular or plural subject.

INSIDE THE SEA OF TRANQUILITY

What will you find inside the Sea of
Tranquility?
Will you find dead bodies of Aliens?
Will you find a village full of people who are purple?
Will you find a blackness that is black as witches?
Will you find water that is gold as King Midas'
daughter?
Will you find Dreams waiting to get out?
Will you find Broken hearts waiting to be healed?
Perhaps you will find . .

— Jamie DelGrosso, Grade 5

THE NIGHTMARE

What will you find in the middle of a
nightmare? You might find goblins, or the devil red
like blood. You might find tragic accidents,
enemies, murderers, your own death,
or a dragon.
I hope the nightmare ends
soon or I wake up. If not I might
get eaten by the dragon.

— Paul Plekon, Grade 5

INSIDE THE MIDDLE
OF AN APPLE

What would you find
in the middle of an apple?
Will you find little people
eating the core like they
never ate before? Will you find
a hole that leads to Disneyland?
Will you find prizes inside
every seed?

— Kathy Lee, Grade 5

SECRETS OF THE HORIZON

What will you find at the end of the horizon?
A sunset?
A fierce wind?
A loud rain?
A full moon?
A bright light?
Nothing at all?
I think you will find a better view
of the world.

— Richard Erhardt, Grade 5

MY SECRET PLACE

This writing exercise speaks for itself, and the best way to set the mood for it with your class is to read sample poems by other children—lots of them—which is why I've included ten. It was especially difficult for me to choose the "Secret Place" samples because I find these poems so winsome they disarm me. They also reflect such a variety of places and reasons for going there that every teacher should find several poems that are exactly right for him or her to read to a class.

1. You might introduce this activity by asking your children to think about a place they like to go when they want to be alone—whether it's to think or read or relax or escape from a bothersome brother or sister.

2. Next put the following titles on the board for the class to think about:

MY SECRET PLACE
MY SPECIAL PLACE
MY HIDING PLACE
MY SPYING PLACE
MY FAVORITE PLACE

I used to naively offer only "My Secret Place" as a topic, but after being asked repeated questions by 2nd Graders–such as: "My place is so secret, how can I tell about it?" or "What if I don't have a secret place?" or "If I tell about my secret place it won't be a secret anymore," I realized I needed to cover all bases. Therefore I was forced to devise the above list, which is practically foolproof, except for the 'secret' part. I solved this by asking all people present to raise right hands and swear after me: "I promise never to tell anyone outside this room about the secret place I might write or hear about."

3. Next I offer the following model:

My _____ Place
is _____
I go there when

_____

I see _____

_____

I hear _____

It makes me feel _____

_____

4. Now read some children's sample poems. Don't hesitate to share a variety of these poems with your class, because one poem example might validate an experience for one child, while a different poem gives the green light to share openly for another.

CHILDREN'S SAMPLE POEMS:

MY SECRET PLACE

My Secret place is a tree
top. I go there with my cousin.
It sounds like a little bird
going through the sky. It
tastes like strawberries.
The leaves are like little men working.
It is scary at night. It looks like a
castle. It makes me
feel like a little man. I love it.
Warren Agostinoni, Grade 2

MY SECRET PLACE

My secret place
is in the woods.
I see birds singing
very pretty.
Pretty leaves are moving
when the wind is
blowing. I can run.
I can breathe in there.
— Michael Vigliante, Grade 2

My secret place
Is in the basement.
It's dark
as a black cat.
And I lock myself in.
It feels like nobody
is there.
Not even me.
— Alex Gomez, Grade 2

THE SPIDERS

My secret place
is a shed where
the spiders are.
the cobwebs are
like clouds.
It feels like dirt
in my shirt. It's
like the spiders are
inside my body
but the big spiders
chew on bugs without
my intention.
— Brandon Alvarez, Grade 2

MY HIDING PLACE

My hiding place is in my room.
I go there only when it is clean.
When the sunshine is through.
It feels warm when I am
still. It reminds me of my
Aunt because she always read
me stories when it was quiet.
I go there when someone hurts
my feelings. My sister Amanda
does not understand my feelings. I
try not to show my feelings but it
does not work. People related to me
try to understand my feelings.
My room is light. I hear the wind
screaming through my ears. When
the wind blows it tastes like
fresh orange juice mixing in flowers.
The wind looks like people
running across the room. It sounds
like racing horses. My Aunt
died but I can remember. In
my hiding place there are open
windows. Sometimes it is cool. It
feels like cold slobbery ice that is
crunching. I like my hiding place
because it reminds me of lots of
things. After my feelings are under
control I go and hug the person that
teased me. I love Amanda anyway.
— Corrie Pickston, Grade 2

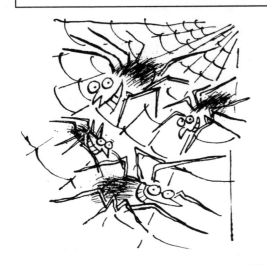

SOMEONE IS CALLING

My secret place is in
my room. I lay down and
I hear my name
    being called in
    the wind "Colleen- - - -
    Colleen." It is
peaceful in my room.
    No one is yelling
    at me. No one
is saying mean things
    about me. It is
nice It is like I
    have a whole different
    house to live in.
    I love myself
    and my family.
— Colleen Kutner, Grade 2

SPECIAL PLACE

My special place
is in the forest I love
to have picnics there
but when I try to
take my friends there
some of them are afraid
of snakes and ticks.
There are wet logs and
gooey leaves sticky
rocks and gross bugs
and I call it Sunshine
Hill cause the sun shines
on the rocks with the
pretty green grass. Sometimes
it rains I have a spot
under a cliff. It is great.
— Kelly McBride, Grade 2

My secret place is in the woods.
I have a place where there is moss
that looks like green green pickles.
There is a cliff that is bumpy
and hard. I sit on the moss.
The wind blows. The leaves in the
trees shiver like Me when I'm cold.
The best time of the month is between April and May. It also has
a stone wall. Fungus grows on it.
My cat, Yougley follows me. His
name is flash like a light or
lightning.

— Katie Schmand, Grade 2

MY HIDING PLACE

My hiding place is in the
closet where my mom and
dad hang their coats. When
I go in there it smells like dirty
stinky shoes. There are spiders
in there but they're dead now
because of the brooms and
coats falling on them. I go
there because I am happy.
I also go there when I play
hide and go seek. My hiding
place is very hot and dark.
Sometimes I wish that it was
a mansion.

— Danielle Pitts, Grade 4

MY SECRET PLACE

My secret place is up in the tree house where
no one ever goes. The trees are like strings all
tangled up. I can see the road and the next
door neighbors. I go up the tree and just sit. It
always is nice when the wind is blowing like
water in a big flood. I go there when I have a
decision to make. I always make the right one when
I'm up there. It makes me want to
stay forever. I feel like an invisible
bird just sitting there. It tastes like water with
anything that gets in it. It makes me feel
like a bird flying away. And then I leave.

— Abby Mennerich, Grade 3

A Final Word

I've had many moving experiences working with children and poetry, and one that sticks with me happened many years ago with a Special Education class of multi-aged youngsters in Trenton, New Jersey. During my entire presentation, on one particular day, a boy in the back of the room kept expressing vehement opposition to poetry and everything connected with it. He hated poems and was not going to lower himself by participating in a writing activity as stupid as this one.

After everyone began to write, the boy reinforced his battle position and leaned his chair back against the wall. He glared at me so fiercely that, naturally, I couldn't wait to work with him. As I approached, he snarled a challenge: "I'm not gonna' do it—so don't waste your time."

"Okay. You don't have to," I replied. "I wouldn't want to waste my time with something I hate, either."

I'd obviously caught him off guard, so I persisted:

"I'm really curious about something. Do you mind if I ask you a question?"

Now he was curious. "All right. One question."

"Why do you hate poetry?"

" 'Cause it's stupid."

"I'm still curious," I continued, "How stupid? Like what?"

He looked surprised. "Are you serious? They won't let me write about nasty stuff."

"Sure you can," I said, noticing his teacher turning pale. "In fact, I'll help you with a first line. Fill in this blank—Poems are_____. Help me finish this!" I implored.

"Poems are garbage," he replied triumphantly.

I wrote "Poems are garbage" on the top of his paper. He looked at me as if I were from Mars.

"Go ahead, be as nasty as you wish. Just be honest."

The boy smiled a little meanly to himself and began to write.

"You're going to hate this!" he chuckled.

This chuckle made me nervous, so I just smiled and backed away slowly so he wouldn't feel pressed. After an audibly gleeful five minutes, the boy (I'll call him Ed) handed me this poem:

> ## GARBAGE
>
> Poems are Garbage.
> Poems are stupid like girls.
> Poems are purple like a rotten banana.
> I hate writing as much as cleaning up the streets.
> I don't like poems because they look like old Bobo's shoes,
> and they're ugly like rotten apples.

After I read it to the class (which Ed didn't think I'd do), his fellow students broke into a spontaneous round of applause. He was, of course, shocked by the acclaim and immediately balled up his creation and threw it into the trash can. I retrieved it, as I have retrieved similarly conceived poems on other occasions, and included it and his next poem—which he surreptitiously handed me the following day—in a small school publication of poetry.

I never saw Ed again, and often wonder what became of him. A part of him will always remain with me, as so many children have stayed with me over the years through the clear and often poignant vision expressed in their poems.

Like so many people, Ed hid his sensitivity and longing for acceptance behind a gruff rejection of poetry and its relevance to his life. He had recognized poetry's "dangerous" language of feeling right away and wanted no part of it.

I'd like to end this book with Ed's second poem, and the hope that more children will realize that even a small moment like this is worth sharing.

> ## THE LEAVES
>
> I was walking down the street and I saw a tree with a whole bunch of leaves and I climbed it to the top and me and the leaves stayed all day long.